THE BOOK OF
FAREHAM

From Market Town to Market Quay

LESLEY BURTON
AND
BRIAN MUSSELWHITE

HALSGROVE

First published in Great Britain in 2006

Copyright © 2006 Lesley Burton and Brian Musselwhite

British Library Cataloguing-in-Publication Data
A CIP record for this title is available from the British Library

ISBN 184114 507 6
ISBN 978 1 84114 507 5

HALSGROVE

Halsgrove House
Lower Moor Way
Tiverton, Devon EX16 6SS
Tel: 01884 243242
Fax: 01884 243325
Email: sales@halsgrove.com
Website: www.halsgrove.com

Frontispiece photograph: *The south side of West Street in the 1970s. Thirty years on, many of these buildings including the venerable Crown inn and the three-storeyed shops still stand, but shoppers now stroll freely where busy traffic once flowed.*

Printed and bound in Great Britain by CPI Bath

Whilst every care has been taken to ensure the accuracy of the information contained in this book, the publisher disclaims responsibility for any mistakes which have been inadvertently included.

Contents

	Acknowledgements	4
Chapter 1	Fareham Then and Now: An Introduction	5
Chapter 2	Views from the Past	13
Chapter 3	The Romance of Cams Hall	23
Chapter 4	Some Fareham Churches	29
Chapter 5	Fareham's Lost Industries	37
Chapter 6	Sea and Quay	45
Chapter 7	Titchfield and the Earls of Southampton	53
Chapter 8	Education and Children	59
Chapter 9	Railway Delights and Road Disasters	69
Chapter 10	Leisure and Pleasure	81
Chapter 11	Caring for the Sick	91
Chapter 12	Fareham and the Second World War	99
Chapter 13	Childhood Memories of Portchester and Fareham by Pam Webb	111
Chapter 14	The Buildings of Fareham	117
Chapter 15	Town in Transition	127
Chapter 16	To the Millennium and Beyond	139
Chapter 17	Some Fareham Personalities	149
	Bibliography	157
	Subscribers	158

Acknowledgements

The authors would like to express their thanks to the many local people who have given valuable advice, support and access to information to enhance the writing of this book. Mr and Mrs C. Hawkins, Mr and Mrs M. Garrett, Mr and Mrs R. Temple and Mr and Mrs J. Ward have kindly provided family photographs and reminiscences. We are also grateful to the staff of Westbury Manor Museum, particularly Julie Biddlecombe, and the staff of Fareham Library. In addition we would like to thank Mike Maude-Roxby, Fareham Borough Council's Conservation Manager, Brenda Clapperton of the Fareham Society, Parallel Business Centres at Cams Hall, Rod Chadwick of HMS Collingwood, Terry Hinckley, John Peters of the Gosport Society and Mr and Mrs C. Brookes for the loan of pictures and slides. George Millener, Mr and Mrs Auld, Peggy Worlock and Pam Webb have kindly helped to identify details on various photographs. We hope you will enjoy Pam Webb's childhood memories of wartime Fareham and Portchester. To all of you we extend our grateful thanks, for without your help much of this community history could not have been written.

Every effort has been made to check copyright for the images appearing in this book. The majority of them come from the Westbury Manor Museum or private collections; we sincerely apologise if any person or organisation has been overlooked.

Lesley Burton and Brian Musselwhite, 2006

Right: *St Peter and St Paul's Church between the wars, featuring the fine bell tower.*

Below: *Buses and charabancs have brought a large Bank Holiday crowd into Wickham Square in the late 1930s.*

✣ CHAPTER 1 ✣

Fareham Then and Now: An Introduction

An engraving, c.1860, entitled View of Fareham from Wallington Hill. *The houses along High Street are prominent in the centre, while the railway viaduct can be seen on the left. The Parish Church rises above the houses, while the spire of Holy Trinity church is in the distance.*

The ancient port and market town once known as Ferneham is barely recognisable today in the large conurbation that is modern Fareham. It has always been quite different from its near neighbours, Portsmouth and Gosport. From the seventeenth century, because of their position at the mouth of Portsmouth Harbour, both these towns were heavily defended with ramparts and moats and were the first line of defence against invasion from France. They also provided protection for the great dockyard, the pride of the Navy for many centuries. High in the north-west corner of the harbour, Fareham was unconfined by the necessity to build barracks and fortifications. For many centuries a market town and a thriving small port with an old-established boat-building industry, its creeks provided a haven for laid-up ships. Fareham, as well as agriculture, had a number of important local industries, as we shall see later.

Since time immemorial the quay has been the point for loading and unloading goods and this continues today, although on a much-reduced scale. A local man who emigrated to Canada in the 1930s revisited Fareham in 1985. At the creek he recalled the big sailing boats of his boyhood days. As they came alongside, he and his friends would climb the masts and enjoy diving into the water.

The town began to acquire the status of desirable residential area towards the end of the eighteenth century. Retired naval officers bought or rented houses in High Street, certain of enjoying a pleasant life with their families in an area not too far removed from the sea but far enough away from the worldly distractions of Portsmouth. At about this time, the people of Fareham started to dabble their toes in the beginnings of the tourist industry. The newspapers of the time inform prospective buyers of the property available and enlighten visitors as to the 'genteel' sea-bathing to be enjoyed in the creek and the good fishing and hunting nearby. The coming of the railways in 1842 brought about the first of many transformations to Fareham's status, not least to the town's economy. Goods from local industries could speedily be whisked away by train to major outlets in the United Kingdom.

From 1850 onwards, local government throughout England was by viable units able to administer the new challenges of increased urbanisation. In 1849

A 1979 view of Fareham, taken from the Civic Centre roof. West Street runs from left to right across the centre, with the Red Lion Hotel on the far left. The much truncated Church Path leads to Quay Street in the centre, with Radford's hardware shop and the Bugle Inn (now named The Brass Monkey) prominent. The creek is quite busy with little craft as it winds around from the recreation ground through the Upper, Town, Lower and Salterns Quays to Fleetlands.

Hamper's boat-building works at Upper Wharf in the 1970s. Although Fareham was not destined to become a commercial port, the various trades connected with its maritime history have been quite prominent over the years. Boat-building, for example, continued well into the late-twentieth century.

Fareham had exchanged its motley collection of bailiffs, constables and a single ale-taster for a Board of Health. Further improvements and modifications resulted in the town becoming an Urban District Council in 1894, which it remained until receiving Borough Council status in 1974.

As with so many other towns up and down the country, the Second World War provided the catalyst for many changes in Fareham. Before 1945, Fareham's individually owned shops and its phenomenally popular Monday market were enjoyed by local residents and visitors alike. The subsequent modernisation of West Street in the 1970s and 1980s did not please everybody:

I miss the old shops, particularly the smell of them. When I was a child, I used to walk down Church Path to Pyle's to fetch bread... it always smelled so good there... Fareham used to be an individual town when I was young in the '50s. The little shops were mostly family businesses, they always seemed to know you and give you the time of day. Now it looks like any other town in Britain, the same shops and names you see everywhere else.

But there are more positive views:

Too many people are negative about the big changes of the past 30-odd years. I am 74 and have lived here all my life and I reckon the changes have done the town a lot of good. The shopping precinct is more convenient and comfortable to shop in than what was here before.

Since the mid-1950s Fareham and its development have been under continual and close scrutiny. One of the earliest and most wide-ranging reports is from 1948, when Portsmouth, Southampton and Hampshire County Councils engaged a young London planner, Max Lock, to look at the whole South Hampshire region and make recommendations on the

✣ FAREHAM THEN AND NOW: AN INTRODUCTION ✣

An Edwardian view of Fareham Market, a major livestock and produce event for over a century.

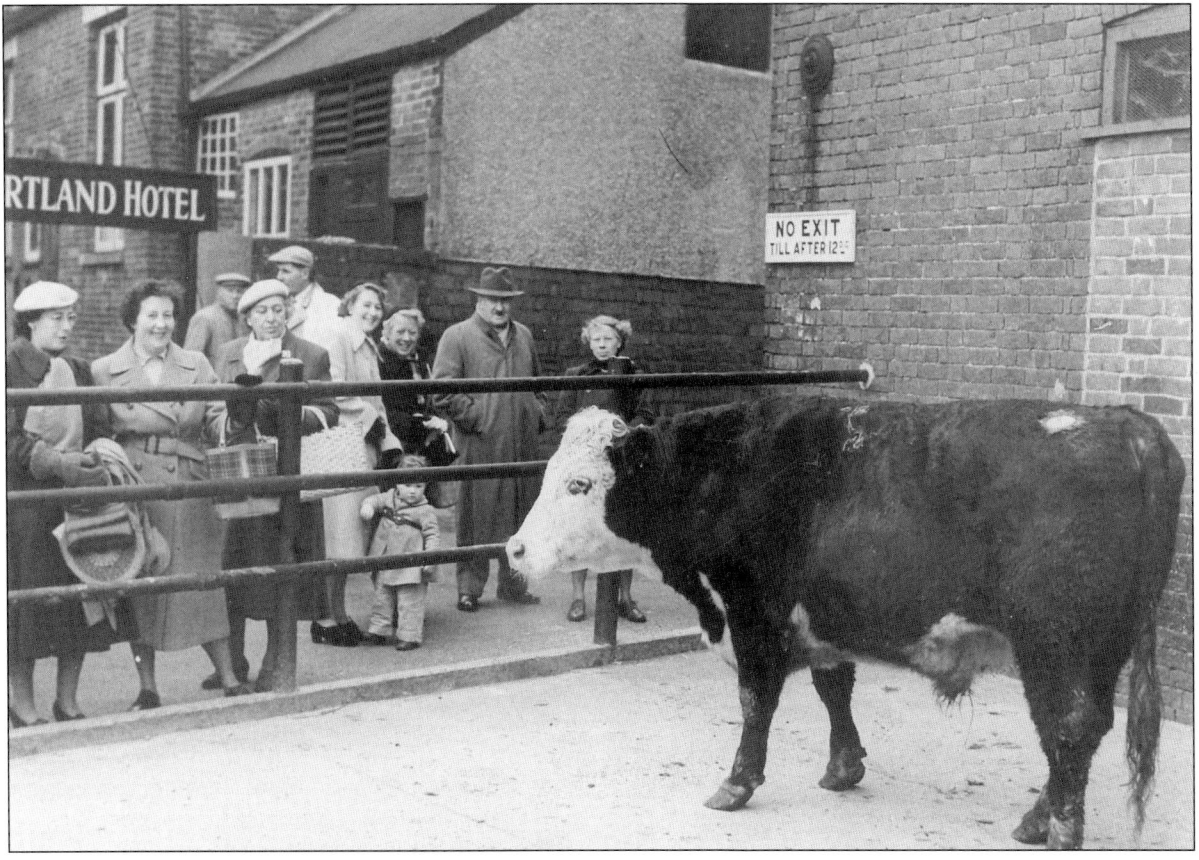

By 1959, when this picture was taken, there were fewer animals to be seen at the weekly market, but this bull has caught the attention of local shoppers.

The twenty-first-century market takes place in the pedestrian area of West Street. Seen here in December 2004, the stalls are somewhat dwarfed by both the new shops (on the left) *and one of the millennium sculptures* (in the foreground).

Fareham has had railway connections since 1841. This unusual view of the main station building was taken in the 1950s.

Fareham station looking north from the footbridge in 1987. The island platform (on the left) *was added in 1889 when a direct route from Southampton via Netley reached the town. The lines straight ahead lead to Eastleigh through the Fareham tunnels.*

The photography and artists' supplies shop of J.T See & Sons was situated on West Street opposite the old Post Office. The See family was prominent in Fareham in various trades for many years.

Cawte's Place in the early 1950s, leading to the little cottages which were characteristic of many of the alleys off West Street at this time. The passageway was earlier known as Coster's Yard.

✦ FAREHAM THEN AND NOW: AN INTRODUCTION ✦

Members of Fareham Fire Brigade in their splendid uniforms, pictured in 1925 outside the fire station in West Street with their first petrol-driven fire engine.

When Miss Matthews was getting married in 1937, she chose Holdaway's of Gosport Road to provide her outfit for the great day. The entire bill for her dress and those of her bridesmaids amounted to just over £5.

An advertisement for J. Herbert Pyle, c.1910. This fine bakery and restaurant served Fareham until the 1960s. Pyle also operated a temperance hotel at No. 161 West Street at the eastern corner of Trinity Street.

From the 1970s much demolition and rebuilding took place in the town centre. One casualty of the changes was this old barn in Quay Street, adjacent to Radford's hardware stores, later G.A. Day's.

The village of Warsash became part of Fareham borough in 1932. This 1983 view of the shoreline shows the unique styling of the harbourmaster's house, which was designed by Hampshire County Council architects.

High Street Post Office in the 1980s. Mr George Clark recalled working there as a boy in the 1920s, selling ice-creams in the summer months.

The same building in December 2005, converted into a private residence.

✣ FAREHAM THEN AND NOW: AN INTRODUCTION ✣

Fareham's modern image. This is West Street in November 2005, looking east with the shopping centre entrances and one of the millennium sculptures on the left.

future provision of the area's economy, transport, education, health and leisure. For Fareham, Lock recommended an increase in population of 11,500 to enhance proposed new industrial outlets and he urged, among many other improvements, the provision of a library and leisure facilities.

Lock also correctly predicted the future huge increase in motor traffic from Gosport through Fareham's 'gateway' at the Lower Quay viaduct. His solution was a new road from Gosport across the upper reaches of the creek joining the A27 at the Delme junction. Quite possibly a financial step too far for the authorities concerned, this, with the benefit of hindsight, was a missed opportunity. 'I like the town centre, it is smart and clean, but the amount of traffic on the roads is a nightmare,' commented a shopper in 2005.

Since the 1960s, the Buchanan Report, various South Hampshire Structure Plans and a never-ending stream of development briefs have been fought over by councillors and the public at large. There was even a campaign for Fareham's amalgamation with Gosport in the 1970s. In fact, until 1974, both towns shared one Member of Parliament.

Fareham's population of 110,000, swollen by the addition of the Western Wards, is now only slightly less than that of the City of Portsmouth. The once outlying villages of Sarisbury, Locks Heath, Park Gate and Whiteley have been the subject of massive developments in housing, light industry and commerce. Only Titchfield, queen of villages, remains relatively untouched.

Fareham today, modern and outward looking, is twinned with Vannes in western France and with Pulheim, a small market town near Cologne, in Germany. More enlightened attitudes to town planning have led to the institution of conservation areas of which, at the time of writing, there are 13, protecting the integrity of Fareham's most interesting historic buildings and open spaces, while the Fareham Society keeps a watchful eye on all planning proposals that they feel would compromise the town's essential character.

In conclusion, we would like to say that this book is not intended as a chronological history of the town. Different readers will be interested in different aspects of Fareham as it has evolved over time. Consequently, the chapters are presented as separate themes to make for easy reading. We hope you will enjoy their content as much as we have enjoyed writing them.

A busy Fareham scene at the end of West Street in the early 1830s. The buildings in the centre of the picture were demolished shortly afterwards, leaving the growing town with a very wide main street.

The eastern end of West Street at the end of the nineteenth century, enhanced with some good new buildings, notably the Portland Hall (on the right) and the neighbouring Congregational Church. By the time this picture was taken the Portland Hall was being used as the Town Hall and as an entertainment venue. The poster advertises the play Mice and Men, *to be performed in aid of the Portsmouth Hospital fund.*

The Portland Hall, originally built in the 1830s to house the meetings of the Society for Literary and Philosophical Objects, has enjoyed a variety of uses over the years. In this picture from the 1980s its imposing façade welcomes customers to the Trustee Savings Bank. Today it is the offices of solicitors Warner, Goodman & Streat.

CHAPTER 2

Views from the Past

Much of Fareham town centre has been transformed since the 1970s by the demolition of old buildings and the erection of new ones. Diggings for the foundations of new structures, together with the excavations which took place to the north of the town when the M27 was being constructed, unearthed remains from the days of our forefathers. A particularly good specimen of medieval ware, a green-glazed jug, was excavated during the development of Market Quay, while the discovery of ancient axes, flints, shards of pottery and coins recalls older eras.

The lives of early societies can, to a large extent, only be a matter of conjecture. The geographical situation of Fareham, however, would have been a promising prospect for settlers. Fertile farming land, well watered and enhanced by a mild climate, was abundant. Portsdown Hill provided shelter from the north-west, while the creeks provided a safe haven for boats. Some 1,000 years ago, Fareham's small community was grouped around the original Church of St Peter and St Paul. The scribes who produced the Domesday Book in 1086 wrote that 'Ferneham', held in demesne by the Bishop of Winchester, consisted of 3,600 acres, a church and two mills, together with a population of 52.

At this time, leading churchmen had great power in Britain, and successive Bishops of Winchester owned vast tracts of land in the south, including the whole of the area around Fareham. By the thirteenth century, the See of Winchester was the richest in the country, owning over 50 manors and boroughs.

Under the method of social organisation known as the feudal system, the bishops and other landowners could demand allegiance from the local peasants, who had to provide goods and services for them through such intermediaries as the lords of the individual manors. In Fareham the local rulers who reported back to the bishop were the Oyselles family at Cams and the Des Roches at Roche Court, who received services from the peasantry and in return granted them the privilege of cultivating small strips of land upon which they grew the crops necessary for their livelihoods. Gradually the feudal system faded away, farming began to be more extensive and the great woodlands of Fareham Park and the Forest of Bere were used for the building of houses and boats. During the fourteenth century, Fareham had grown enough in importance to be granted borough status, together with the right to hold an annual fair. The town was even afforded the honour of sending two burgesses to the early parliament of 1306, a privilege which was lost by 1345, apparently because the town could not afford the expense involved.

No written records survive of visitors' impressions of Fareham in these early times. Indeed, travel for its own sake was a concept unknown to the vast majority of medieval folk; it has been estimated that the average person today encounters more people in a day than a fourteenth century peasant would have met in a lifetime. For the next 200 years we have only snippets of information concerning how Fareham appeared to outsiders. For example, John Leland, librarian to Henry VIII, visited the area at some time between 1531 and 1543 while compiling a topographical account of Britain. With relatively little to report, he describes the scene north of Forton thus:

A myle and a half above this is Bedenham Creeke so caullid of a village standing by it. This creek's mouth lyith almost agayn Portechester Castelle. Fareham a fisscher village lyith about a myle more upward at the very hedde of the haven.

Almost a century later, another report shows the local community in a rather more favourable light. An unknown informant to Sir John Coke, Charles I's Commissioner of the Navy, wrote that:

The river leading to Fareham within a mile of the town is an absolute good and safe place to moor ship and in all respects as convenient and safe a harbour as Chatham. £2000 may be saved the king in moorings and men.

Despite such a good report, Fareham never developed into a naval dockyard, although shipbuilding, which had certainly started up on the shores of the creek, continued well into the last century.

In the eighteenth century that brave and zealous preacher John Wesley travelled the length and breadth of the country bringing the word of God to those ordinary folk neglected by the Church of England. In 1738 he spoke to crowds in Newport, Isle of Wight and, pleased with his reception there, crossed the Solent to visit the Fareham area. To quote from his journal:

On Sunday I preached in the street at Fareham. Many gave great attention but seemed neither to feel nor understand anything.

A few days later, however, he preached again, and

13

This engraving from the 1860s features Holy Trinity Church, set in the newly developing residential area of West Street. Although the picture was made by Newman's of London, it was published locally by Thomas Mansell, whose shop is seen on the right behind the tree.

'a wild multitude was present yet only a few mocked – the greater part were soon deeply attentive.'

From the middle of the eighteenth century onwards, we are fortunate to have the printed directories which were published from time to time. Although the contents of such directories are somewhat variable – some give many details, others are very sketchy concerning the places under discussion – they remain a valuable reference tool. In the *Hampshire Directory* for 1784, many Fareham inhabitants and their trades are listed, the maritime links being reflected in such as Edward Brackstone, shipbuilder, William Chapman, 'master of a Plymouth trader', and Thomas Perry, hoyman. We learn that:

William Saunders, John Pye and Stephen Figg's Boats

The Victorian residences situated along the part of West Street west of Holy Trinity Church had mostly been converted into shops by the 1930s and still function as such today, as this picture from December 2005 shows.

✦ VIEWS FROM THE PAST ✦

More Victorian houses that have become shops, this time along the north side of West Street, pictured here in the 1930s. The clock advertises the premises of Harold Job, a well-known jewellers situated for many years near the corner of Malthouse Lane.

One of Fareham's earlier public buildings, the Connaught Drill Hall, once home to the Territorial Army, in 1981.

Foresters' Hall in 2005, this once-fashionable venue for balls, dances and entertainments now somewhat forlorn and advertised 'To Let'. The stylish sign below proclaims the furniture store of Birks, a family firm which has served Fareham for over 80 years.

go every morning to Portsmouth, and return in the Evening – Fare three-pence per Head.

The directory provides evidence of the early development of Fareham's industries – Arthur Coster is listed as a pipe-maker, Stephen Fitchett as a timber-merchant and Mary and Henry Franklin as basket-makers. Coach-building, later to bring the town some fame when the Coles family's West Street factory produced vehicles for royalty, was at this time carried out by John Jurd who, no doubt, was assisted by wheelwrights William Jurd and Hayter Kinch, together with blacksmiths William Merrett and John Stokes and ironmonger John Strugnell. Edward Webb is listed as a brick-burner, Richard Wells as a cabinet-maker and William and John Thresher as tanners. In those days, before the railway appeared on the scene, long-distance travel was by passenger coach, while goods were conveyed in heavy horse-drawn wagons; those coaches which left from Gosport to travel to London all called at John Hunt's Royal Oak inn to pick up passengers or parcels.

15

The fine vista of Osborn Road looking west in the 1980s. Behind the walls and trees stand some of Fareham's finest buildings, erected under the aegis of Charles Osborn in mid-Victorian days.

Part of Osborn Road, the flint walls of which now rather incongruously face the entrance to the severely functional multi-storey car park. Osborn Road has been designated a conservation area by Fareham Borough Council.

Post-chaises could be hired from Thomas Hewitt at the Red Lion Hotel and Thomas Frost at the Bugle. Such activity, together with quite a large number of individual shops ranging from Peter Hillyer and John Prior, gingerbread-makers, to James Stubbington, bookseller and stationer, indicates a busy and vigorous town at this time.

Warner's *History of Hampshire*, published in 1795, gives a more detailed impression of Fareham at the end of the eighteenth century.

The soil is generally rich and the county affords plenty of cattle, wool, bacon, wood, iron and honey. The sea coast here furnishes lobsters, oysters and other sea fish and its rivers abound in fresh fish, especially trout. The farmers are a substantial class of men, full of agricultural knowledge and industry. They are very fond of fine teams of horses, each vies with his neighbour to outdo him in having better cattle. Fareham is a pleasant town, with a market on Tuesdays and a fair on June 29th. It has a well-endowed Charity School where children are instructed to read and write so as to qualify them for useful employment in life. King Charles II dignified this place with the honourary title of an earldom in creating Madame de Queroval, his mistress, Countess of Fareham. Cams, south-east of Fareham, is the elegant seat of the family of Delme.

The June fair mentioned by Warner was probably the favourite social occasion of the year for local people. Over the years it developed from a horse-trading and farm produce fair into a larger festival encompassing rides, peepshows and entertainments of all kinds. The venue was High Street, although at times stalls and rides spilled over into West Street, and in the nineteenth century the fair was marked by processions through the town, culminating in water sports at the creek. At one time, the fair became particularly well known for the amount and variety of cheeses on sale. Eventually, however, the annual fair fell into decline, the last one being held in 1871.

At the beginning of the nineteenth century, the centre of the developing town was around the eastern end of West Street. The fine houses in High Street, then known as North Street, led up to the Church of St Peter and St Paul, which marked the northern edge of Fareham. Overlooked by the Red Lion Hotel, the eastern end of West Street contained tightly packed houses and shops, some of them in little alleys off the main road. East Street led away to the turnpike gate, while Quay Street, busy with little houses and workshops, led south to the town's boundary on the road to Gosport; there were a few residences further along West Street and up Puxhold Lane. When the novelist William Makepeace Thackeray stayed as a child in the 1820s at his great-grandmother's cottage in West Street, adjacent to what became Portland Street, Fareham left its mark on him. In later life he recalled it as:

... a dear little old Hampshire town inhabited by the wives, widows, daughters of navy captains, admirals, lieutenants.

In 1830, Pigott's *Directory of Hampshire* affirms Thackeray's observations. Fareham, he writes, 'is eligibly situated on an arm of the sea and chiefly inhabited by persons of maritime occupation.' Pigott goes on to mention Palmeter's floating dock, Burrell's marine stores, the trade by sea of coal, corn and wood, as well as the developing earthenware and brick-making industries and Bartholomew's ironworks.

At this time, some of Fareham's older buildings were replaced by more substantial brick constructions. One building in particular added architectural style to the town. This was the fine Portland Hall, erected in the 1850s on behalf of the Society for Literary and Philosophical Objects. This particular society did not last long, but the hall has seen many and varied uses over the years; variously a corn exchange, a town hall and the venue for balls, dances and entertainments. In 2006 it is a splendid home to a firm of solicitors. Other impressive buildings, erected a few years later, included two large churches, the Independent Chapel (later to become the United Reformed Church) and Holy Trinity itself, further along West Street, both of which were probably the work of the architect Jacob Owen. A much more mundane structure was the new gasworks by the creek, which nevertheless provided the means for the main streets to be lit for the first time with gas. In 1840 the contributor to Mudie's *Hampshire* book commented enthusiastically about Fareham:

It is a great thoroughfare by land and a seaport to a very extensive district. For local trade it is indeed much better situated than Portsmouth itself.

In the same year, Robson's *Directory of Hampshire* mentioned a new development at Fareham:

During the summer months it has a large influx of visitors for the benefit of sea-bathing, and a commodious bathing-house has been erected for their accommodation.

The arrival of the railway – of which more in another chapter – effected not only social changes but also had a considerable physical impact upon the town. The extension of the line from Fareham to Portsmouth in 1848 necessitated the erection, across the southern part of the town and over the inlets of the creek, of a magnificent many-arched viaduct, the massive presence of which, now paralleled by a wide road, acts almost as a boundary wall behind which the modern town is contained.

Another major development at the beginning of the second half of the nineteenth century was the construction of the Maindell water pumping station, which improved the town's water supplies and sanitation needs thanks to the building of a new reservoir near Fort Wallington. Cravet's *Directory of Hampshire* enthused:

Fareham is a railway town and has within late years made great advances, for fifty years ago it was merely a village, the houses only cottages; this improvement is chiefly owing to John Barney Esq. (of 'Lysses', High Street) who pulled down the old buildings and erected more modern and handsome structures. There is a considerable manufacture of red clay pottery, established by Mr Thomas Stares of Wallington, nearly the whole of the western counties being supplied. The exports from the town are oak timber, bark, hoops, pottery and bricks.

By 1861 Fareham's population had grown to a substantial 11,000. William White's *Hampshire* book of this year provided a directory of inhabitants of the town together with their professions. Fareham had two each of chemists, butchers, tallow chandlers, cabinet-makers, ironmongers and hairdressers. There were four each of bakers, milliners, watch and

When the railways reached Fareham, the Red Lion Hotel, almost a mile from the station, began to provide a 'courtesy coach' to transport patrons, as this late Victorian photograph shows.

High Street at its junction with West Street at the turn of the century. On the left is E.&C. Hunt's Fareham Cycle Works, which produced the 'Swallow' range of bicycles. Next door is W.G. Abraham, upholsterer and cabinet maker, which proudly announces services going back to 1837.

Fort Wallington Tavern, c.1900. Soldiers stationed during the nineteenth century at Fort Wallington had plenty of time on their hands, and no doubt were frequent visitors here. Supplies from Blake's brewery of Gosport have been unloaded from the cart.

❖ VIEWS FROM THE PAST ❖

This part of High Street was known as Vicar's Hill. The old cottages are now gone, although the Post Office building remains and is a private dwelling.

The narrow thoroughfare of Union Street, looking towards High Street, in December 2005. In the early-nineteenth century, Fareham Union Workhouse was situated here; a new one was built on the Wickham Road in 1836.

Colenso Road, December 2005. One of the town's small areas of older housing quite near to the busy shopping area of West Street, its unusual name probably commemorates the Boer War battle of Colenso.

Quay Street, once known as South Street, disgorges traffic from the Quay roundabout into the far eastern end of West Street in December 2005. The large corner building, a specialist hardware store throughout the twentieth century, was replaced in 2005 by the Indian restaurant seen here.

clock makers and greengrocers, while there were no fewer than six grocers and boot and shoe manufacturers. Fresh bread was provided in the establishments of Jonathan Pannell, Charles Pargent and George Pink. James Buckett and Thomas Howard provided wares for the newly fashionable habit of smoking, while George Boorn and David Harris offered wines and spirits. George Cole's coach-building factory in West Street might well have displayed the royal coat of arms, as it was patronised by Queen Victoria and had earlier served William IV. Cole employed 30 workmen and proudly advertised the fact that the firm exported carriages as far afield as Australia. Other establishments, too, catered for the needs of horse-drawn transport: Robert Bruce, Edward Windsor and Thomas Hoare were blacksmiths in West Street, John Dean was a wheelwright and Joseph Hoare, Daniel Pargent and William Pink were saddlers.

Throughout the latter half of the nineteenth century Fareham was gradually provided with those amenities and improvements which typified the development of Victorian towns. Electric lights replaced gas lighting in the main streets as early as 1890, the current originally carried along overhead cables from the new generating station built at Lower Quay. By 1894 Fareham had become an urban district council, meetings being held at the Portland Hall. The town had had a police service, stationed at Osborn Road, since 1854, and by the end of the century the staff consisted of superintendent Mr W. Hack, a sergeant and five officers. In 1888 the fire service, originally operating from High Street, found a new home in Quay Street, although it was to be moved again to a new building in West Street, next to the Market Hall, in 1910.

As the twentieth century dawned, Fareham's mile-long West Street was almost completely built up. Besides residences and shops both large and

THE BOOK OF FAREHAM

A fine view looking east from the roof of the Civic Centre in June 1979. A century before, almost all the fine buildings along High Street would have been upper-class residences; most are now shops and restaurants or other businesses. Lysses House, now a hotel, is prominent on the left. In the top right of the picture, the railway viaduct carries the lines to Portsmouth over the River Wallington and Portchester Road. Note the fascinating variety of roofs and frontages of the High Street buildings.

Amid the bustle of redevelopment that has transformed much of the town centre, many interesting old buildings remain in situ. *The elegant edifice in the centre of this photograph from 2005 houses Stephen's the barbers, with a beauty salon above. The archway leads to Hewlett's Court. Where the modern shop of Ethel Austin now stands there was once a Tudor building that housed Hayward's the greengrocers, together with a larger establishment which was formerly Hinxman's garage.*

❖ VIEWS FROM THE PAST ❖

In December 2005 we see a mixture of building styles and periods. The 'Horn of Plenty' sculpture of 2000 stands in front of the nineteenth-century Crown public house, which temporarily sports a twenty-first century Father Christmas. In the background, the shop trading under the very modern name 'Nailz Inc' displays a plaque of Queen Victoria prominently on the side of the building.

In November 2004 a shopper contemplates the variety of flowers on sale in front of Fareham's new Market Quay shops; the banner advertises the Ferneham Hall pantomime Cinderella *and shopfitters work inside what is shortly to become a branch of Robert Dyas, the hardware store.*

small, it also now boasted the 1881-built Foresters' Hall and, on the opposite side of the road, Connaught Hall; these two, together with Holy Trinity Church Hall, Portland Hall and the Red Lion Hotel, were used for various social functions. The preferred housing areas for the better off were High Street, Southampton Road and Osborn Road, while away from the town centre such large houses as Heathfield House, Elm Villa, Belvoir, Southfield House and Blackbrook House were the residences of the wealthy. Osborn Road, now denoted a conservation area by Fareham Borough Council, was developed by Charles Osborn of Down End House. He planned a group of houses which would form a vista to the Church of St Peter and St Paul, and built the two roads which bore his name – Osborn Road and Charles Street (now Osborn Road South). The first houses to be built were the vicarages for the Church of St Peter and St Paul and for Holy Trinity. Next came Ellesmere House and further elegant mansions, all enclosed within flint boundary walls.

Fareham's industries, including brick-making, pottery and tanning, were flourishing, while the quays still saw plenty of commercial use, with trading vessels of every kind and workshops relating to marine activities, besides the large steam-driven flour mill. With farming, still a major force in the area, becoming more organised, in 1891 a number of local agriculturalists founded the Fareham and Hampshire Farmers' Club to promote co-operation and discussion among its members, to gain a wider knowledge of new farming methods and machinery and to lobby the government in the hope of affording some protection from cheap foreign food imports. The first President was J. Carpenter-Garnier of Rookesbury Farm, Wickham, the first secretary was R. Burrill, and by 1898 the club had over 300 members. Meanwhile, the market, often a somewhat haphazard affair, was reorganised into a more coherent weekly event by a group of farmers in conjunction with Austin & Wyatt, the High Street auctioneers. This market company bought the land south of West Street which became the official market place, although for many years afterwards animals were still driven through the streets from local fields or along West Street from the railway station. In the twenty-first century, the Monday market has reverted once again to West Street – although the bleating, neighing and mooing have long since been replaced by the cries of street traders!

✦ CHAPTER 3 ✦

The Romance of Cams Hall

Cams Hall, viewed from the south-east in 1894.

A view of Cams Hall from the south.

The entire area we recognise today as the former Cams Hall estate is as old as the Domesday Book and at that time was under the jurisdiction of the Bishop of Winchester. Acquired 100 years later by Robert Oysell, he gave it the name Cammes Oysell, the property remaining with the family until 1397. For the next three centuries several landed families held sway at Cams, enlarging the estate and adding farmhouses to the original manor. At the time of the Civil War, the Badd family were in residence. An enthusiastic Royalist, Thomas Badd, who had been created Baron in 1642, set about enlarging the original magnificent manor of Cams. At this period, if the tax returns of 1665 are anything to go by, it was clearly an imposing house and is credited with having a total of 15 hearths or fireplaces.

After Badd's death in 1682 the manor house and estate were bought by Richard Chandler, ownership staying with this family for three generations. Put up for sale in 1767, Cams was purchased by Sir Jacob Wolff, by which time the estate comprised the original manor house, a mansion house, farmhouses and 500 acres of woodlands and pasture land. The eighteenth century would see Cams enter the most flourishing period of its existence. Sir Jacob Wolff spent a total of just three years in residence before selling to Brigadier-General Carnac, at that time the Member of Parliament for Leominster. Carnac, previously a senior official with the East India Company, now took the decision to demolish the manor house and build in its stead a spacious new house on the shores of Fareham creek. Carnac chose as his architect the up-and-coming Jacob Leroux, known to him through their service with the East India Company. Leroux had received acclamation for his design work at Southampton, including York Buildings and the combination of houses, public buildings and gardens known as the Polygon. Before his work at

An early-twentieth-century view of Cams Hall. After 1894 the house gradually deteriorated as successive owners were unable to finance the necessary repairs.

The library at Cams Hall, 1894.

Another book-lined room at Cams Hall.

Southampton, the youthful Leroux had served time as a pupil with the architect of the East India Company's headquarters in London's Leadenhall Street. This building was demolished in 1862 but a blue plaque records its former presence.

Leroux's Cams Hall building is substantially the one we see today. Classically styled in Portland stone, in the rural Fareham of two and a half centuries ago it would have seemed even more remarkable than it does today, bordered by woodland and, to the south, the calm waters of the creek. By 1777, however, General Carnac had moved on and the sparkling new building was put on the market for the enormous price, for that period, of £17,000. The buyer attracted to this grand property, and who had the money to pay for it, was Peter Delme, whose family would be in residence for nearly 120 years.

Peter Delme must be one of the most interesting upwardly mobile gentlemen ever to be associated with Fareham. The Delmes were a Walloon family originating from the province of Lorraine in northern France and were of mixed Belgian and French ancestry. Like the Huguenots, they were subjected to religious persecution in the sixteenth and seventeenth centuries. Many fled to England, in particular to the prosperous wool towns of Southampton and Norwich, and it is at Norwich that the first immigrant Delme, Adrian, is recorded in 1589 as holding the office of deacon of the Walloon church in the city. Over the next 200 years the Delmes prospered by marrying into the landowning English aristocracy. In time another Delme, Pierre, would become director of the fledgling Bank of England and, in 1723, Lord Mayor of London.

The Cams Hall Delme was one of Pierre's grandsons. Peter Delme, born on 19 December 1748, grew to be an ambitious young man, possibly trying to

A room at Cams Hall showing the marble columns and moulded ceilings typical of the building in the nineteenth century.

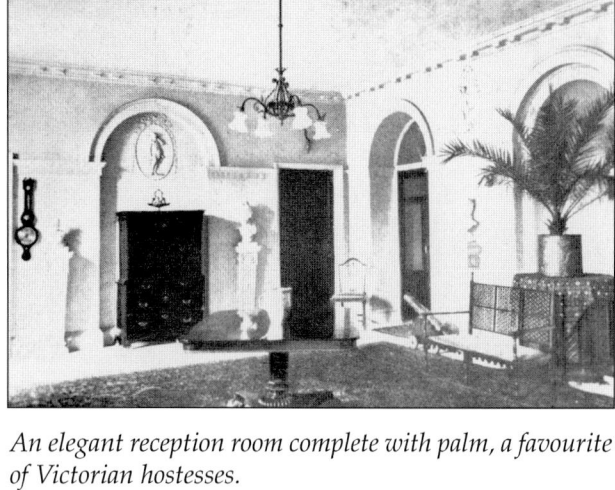
An elegant reception room complete with palm, a favourite of Victorian hostesses.

The kitchen at Cams Hall, somewhat primitive by today's standards.

emulate his grandfather and to prove that a wealthy immigrant family could move through society with the best of the English aristocracy. He appears to have had the skills for forming friendships in high places. Two months after his twenty-first birthday, in 1769, he married Lady Elizabeth Howard, third daughter of the fourth Duke of Carlisle. Lady Elizabeth was a 'catch' and a noted beauty who, in 1777, would sit for the artist Sir Joshua Reynolds. This splendid portrait, which included two of the five Delme children, graced the walls of Cams Hall until 1894, when it was sold at auction at Christies for the then enormous sum of £11,000. Peter Delme's marriage brought him into the highest reaches of Georgian society, his wife being one of the ladies-in-waiting to George III's Queen, Charlotte. Through this connection Peter Delme made the acquaintance of the Prince Regent. Although endowed with the considerable inherited wealth of his father and grandfather, Peter Delme could only realise his desire to enter Parliament through the political patronage of his father-in-law, the Duke of Carlisle. This was given and Peter Delme was elected Member of Parliament for Morpeth in 1774, when he was only 26 years old. He remained Morpeth's representative until his death in 1789.

At the time of his purchase of Cams Hall, Peter Delme and his growing family were living at the magnificent Place House, Titchfield, and it is not exactly clear why he should have wished to leave there. One possible reason is that, for a Member of Parliament, Cams Hall would have made for an easier commute to London, especially with the new turnpike roads. Another reason may have been that the remoteness of Place House denied the easy access to London society to which Lady Elizabeth was accustomed. Furthermore, a great deal of work would have been necessary to maintain the ancient fabric of Place House when compared with a virtually new house such as Cams Hall.

Once ensconced at Cams Hall, Peter Delme systematically plundered much of the inner structure and fittings of Place House in order to enhance his new home. Marble fireplaces, columns, cornices and statuary were stripped and transferred to Cams Hall. It was, in a practical sense, asset-stripping of the worst kind. Fortunately for posterity, some of these original fittings survive: they were salvaged from Cams Hall and, at the time of writing, are on display at Westbury Manor Museum.

Peter Delme's son, John, succeeded his father and added to the glamour of the hall by installing further high-quality fittings, many by the Adam brothers. At the age of 19, John had married Frances Garnier of Rookesbury Park. During both Peter and John Delmes's tenure, the estate was greatly increased. The lodges and the long, sweeping drive

The Oval Room, ready for use at a conference. Compare this with the same room in 1894 (top left).

The Bailiff's House at Cams Hall, 1894.

up to the front of the house, as well as the screen wall which hid the home farm complex, were the inspiration of Peter Delme. It is also believed that the brickwork on the curving south wall of the hall was the work of Delme senior.

Cams Hall was at the height of its architectural magnificence at a critical period in England's history. Ships waited on the alert at Portsmouth at a time when a possible invasion from France loomed. Many admirals would have dined at Cams Hall, possibly Lord Nelson among them. Jane Austen's two naval brothers, Francis and Charles, were very familiar with Fareham and there were ships of the line moored in Fareham creek. Officers of His Majesty's Navy may very well have sat around the dining table with the Delmes and eaten exotic fruits gathered from the estate's hothouses. It would, in time, prove to be Cams Hall's tragedy that most of family's male members died young. John Delme died aged 36, though not before producing a formidable tally of 11 children. All seven of his sons were childless and his eldest, John, died when he was only 23 years old.

An 1894 view of the Cams Hall stables.

✣ THE ROMANCE OF CAMS HALL ✣

Above: *Cams Hall restored to its eighteenth-century magnificence and now a Grade II listed building.*

Left: *The south elevation showing the rounded bay which is echoed in various other buildings in Fareham.*

The last remaining Delme, Seymour Robert, died in 1894 aged 86, at which time the estate was put up for sale. The auctioneers, King & King, were charged with marketing Cams Hall, and the catalogue description, which is positively lyrical, also impresses on prospective buyers the many advantages of its location, in particular the good connections to London by rail.

Charmingly situated on the southern slope of the Portsdown range, within six miles of the naval port and garrison town of Portsmouth and Southsea, close to the market and Post and Telegraph town of Fareham with the station on the London and South Western Railway and two and a half hours journey to the capital... the Lodge gives on to beautifully timbered parks, gently undulating towards the south, securing charming views over Portsmouth Harbour, the Solent and the Isle of Wight... packs of hounds within easy distance.

Buyers are informed of the 30 rooms and additional quarters for servants, a huge conservatory with tiled floor and a fountain on the south-facing lawns. And there is much, much more. Farms, orchards, a rookery, a wilderness, north and south parks, stabling and coachhouses and the profitable home farm. Alas, the auctioneers' hype came to nothing. A year later, the local press announced that East Cams Farm had been disposed of and the home portion was again put up for sale. This included the mansion, grounds and parks plus much agricultural land, a total of 250 acres. A dismal £10,250 was paid by the new owner, Montague Foster of Stubbington House School, who let the estate out to tenants over the next 30 or so years. In 1933 the building and contracting firm of Jonathan May & Sons bought Cams Hall with the intention of building houses on the site. The outbreak of the Second World War precluded this as all viable agricultural land was required by the government for intensive food production. In 1939 the Admiralty took over the house and the estate and did not vacate it until 1950.

Between the wars, gunnery practice at Whale Island disturbed the peace and security of the tenants when shot occasionally landed on the south lawns. A much more serious incident occurred on 14 July 1950, when ammunition barges at the Royal Naval Armament Depot in Gosport blew up, causing a massive explosion and sending shock waves around the harbour which loosened the ceilings and damaged the inner fabric of the Hall. In 1951 Cams Hall was again auctioned off, this time to a company who left it to deteriorate further. Vandals stripped lead off the roof and made off with many of the fittings. Although Fareham Urban District Council was keen to buy the building, no government loan was available. Another interested party was Hampshire County Council, which bought part of the grounds to develop Fareham Grammar School for Girls. Other parts of the land were given over to caravanning and to agricultural use. In 1977 outline planning permission was given by the new Fareham Borough Council for partial demolition of the by now badly decayed house. Developers with assorted proposals now came thick and fast and both the Council and the objectors were permanently at loggerheads. A severe fire in 1981 threatened Cams Hall and set alight woodlands. The local architectural practice of Hedley Greentree proposed a viable scheme which involved

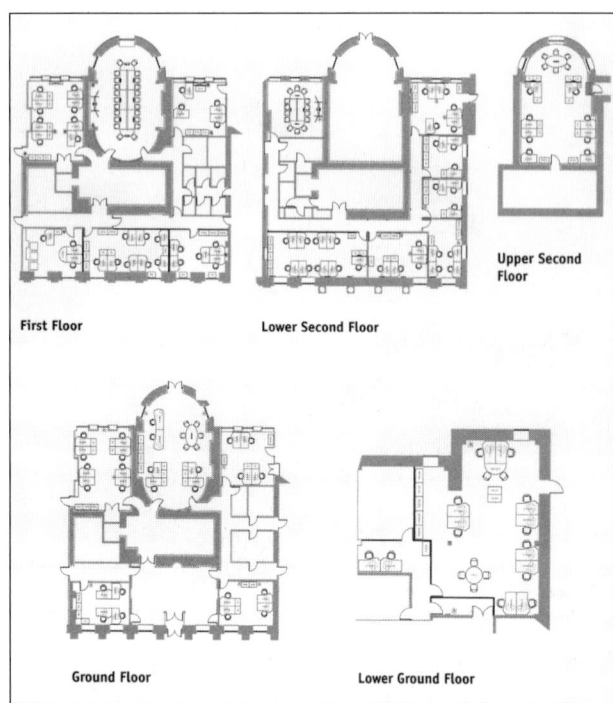

The plans of the buildings show the characteristic shapes of the rooms at Cams Hall. The largest room is used for receptions and conferences.

a large-scale business park with a golf course as an attractive leisure amenity. Councillors disapproved; it might turn out to be, in the words of one of them, 'a mini-IBM'. The scheme was thrown out and, somewhat belatedly, the Council recommended that the entire Cams estate, or what remained of it, should be declared a conservation area and work done to improve the landscape of the deteriorating site.

A second application from Hedley Greentree got a more favourable reception, this time from Fareham Borough Council, but a stop was put on the scheme as a result of the wild life discovered in residence in the Hall. Bats had been found, a threatened species, and a series of consultations with local bat groups ensued. When the solution was found in favour of both the hall and the bats, the Cams jinx struck again when an objector from Hampshire County Council cited the Fareham Review of the Town Map in 1968, claiming that even Hedley Greentree's scaled-down proposal was an over-intensive use of a sensitive site.

Strand Harbour Securities and Warings of Portsmouth purchased the estate in 1991 and commenced the immediate restoration of the hall and the remaining 180 acres of the site. Fareham Borough Council agreed with the company that it should be given a new lease of life but with no extensions to the original fabric or any significant alterations to the façade. The restoration took five years and cost over £4 million. A computer firm, LAVA UK, which took over the hall for a lease of 15 years, quickly went into receivership. At the time of writing Parallel Business Centres run Cams Hall as serviced offices offering high-tech workshop space and much besides. The adjoining popular golf course provides wonderful views across and around the creek.

Cams Hall today is like the proverbial sleeping beauty, aroused from a century of slumber plagued with nightmares of decay, ruin, controversy and the tragic death of a site worker from electrocution. Although only a few of the magnificent interiors of Peter Delme's time remain, externally there is much to enjoy. The people of Fareham can gaze at the handsome Portland stone façade and welcome back Cams Hall – a much-loved old neighbour with a new lease of life.

Newlyweds Heather and Peter Coates Buglear pose by their vintage Rolls-Royce in the late 1990s. The timeless elegance of Cams Hall provides a splendid backdrop for wedding ceremonies and receptions.

❖ CHAPTER 4 ❖

Some Fareham Churches

The impressive Parish Church of St Peter and St Paul, viewed from Osborn Road, December 2005.

The church has always played a prominent part in Fareham's history. The Parish Church, dedicated to St Peter and St Paul, existed in much smaller form, on the same site, as early as the time of the Domesday Book of 1086. In the twenty-first century, Fareham has a large and varied number of places of worship, the membership and vigour of which quite buck the present trend away from attendance at religious institutions.

The site of the Church of St Peter and St Paul, somewhat distant from what may be considered the main part of the modern town, hints that the medieval settlement of Fareham was concentrated mostly in the High Street area in the days before the causeway over the Wallington river was built.

The church has been rebuilt on several occasions and today only one chancel survives from medieval times. The solid Georgian tower was constructed in 1742, its base made of stone taken from the earliest

The south aspect of the Church of St Peter and St Paul, February 2005.

building, the rest of local bricks. Three years later, the church had a belfry with a weather vane on top and a set of eight bells. The town grew and, by 1812, major rebuilding was deemed necessary, the nave

29

Originally built at the highest point in the town, the Church of St Peter and St Paul dominated Fareham's skyline until the erection of the civic buildings in the late 1970s. This view from the roof of the Civic Centre in June 1979, shows the southern side and roof of the church, now far below, together with High Street with Lysses in the centre and the back of the Golden Lion inn on the far right.

The former Parish Church vicarage, built by Charles Osborn and now an official residence for the Bishop of Portsmouth.

being extended and only the tower and chancel left as they were. The re-hung bells were supplemented by two new ones in the early 1880s. In 1888 church architect Sir Arthur Blomfield was appointed to redesign the church. Under his aegis a new chancel was built and the older one restored as a side chapel, while an alabaster pulpit was added as a memorial to the former vicar, Revd W.S. Dumergue.

Throughout the twentieth century, further changes and improvements were made, culminating in the fine interior that worshippers enjoy today. Sir Charles Nicholson made major changes in 1930, altering the nave by removing the galleries and wooden pillars and constructing new arches. He also introduced a wooden ceiling decorated with coloured shields depicting the keys of St Peter and the sword of St Paul. The fine interior of the building was seen by a greater number of people than usual when the church was featured on television. In March 1979 Southern Television broadcast a Lent service led by the vicar, Revd Leslie Chadd, and in the following year the popular BBC series *Songs of Praise* featured the church and included music from the Fareham Philharmonic Society conducted by Brian Hall, with Nigel Smith at the organ.

Undoubtedly, the Church of St Peter and St Paul is one of Fareham's finest architectural treasures and, although it no longer dominates the skyline – the civic centre offices building dwarfs it – it retains a quiet, tranquil spirit. Today it is Fareham's other large Anglican church, Holy Trinity, which is more prominent, standing as it does in the middle of West Street. Holy Trinity was first conceived as a chapel-at-ease to alleviate growing problems with regard the space available at the Church of St Peter and St Paul. During the 1830s the number of pews there was proving inadequate, many of them being privately owned by local people who paid handsomely for the privilege, while others were rented out to families of high social standing, many of whom were not even Fareham residents. This situation, together with the growth of population in Fareham's west end, led to the church elders deciding, in 1832, to build an additional chapel 'as affording the greater accommodation for the poor'. Sir Henry Thompson, a curate

SOME FAREHAM CHURCHES

Holy Trinity church in West Street, pictured in the 1980s. Built in 1835, the church was originally a chapel-at-ease for the Parish Church.

at St Peter and St Paul, was a prominent supporter of the proposed new chapel.

His mother, Dame Jane Thompson, widow of Admiral Sir Charles Thompson and a local benefactor, had bought a site in Puxol Lane with a view to erecting the suggested new church there. When she died the following year, bequeathing this site in her will, the church authorities decided to sell it and use the money to buy a different plot of land along West Street. This consisted of:

120 feet of Garden Ground now in the occupation of Mr Gills, together with half an acre of land at the back thereof, the property of Mrs Woolls, as a site for the erection of a Church.

A subscription list opened, headed by Sir Henry Thompson, which included contributions from such local worthies as Isaac Kiln, Robert James, Richard Clark and Messrs J. and S. Burrell. The new church was built by local men working under Thomas Fulford and John Palmer, local carpenters and masons who had also contributed to the funds. In December 1835 the new church, consecrated by Bishop Sumner, was described as 'an edifice in brick, with stone dressings, in the Gothic style.' Two years later the western tower, complete with spire, was added. The first incumbent of Holy Trinity was Sir Henry Thompson, assisted by Captain Borlase and William Spain as churchwardens.

The new church was well attended. An early event in its life was a special celebration for the coronation of Queen Victoria in June 1838. A thanksgiving service was followed by a procession along West Street and what were quaintly termed 'rustic amusements' for the locals. Fareham children were offered a meal consisting of roast beef, a penny roll, plum pudding and half a pint of beer.

By 1846 Holy Trinity had become a separate parish, the rectory being built two years later. Between 1847 and 1855, the vicar was Revd Edward Lyon Berthon, one of those energetic and indefatigable churchmen–visionaries of the Victorian era whose interests and imagination knew no bounds. Besides his vigorous efforts to improve both the spiritual and temporal lot of his parishioners, Berthon studied medicine and theology, travelled widely at home and abroad and worked on innovative maritime projects, inventing a collapsible boat which was demonstrated before the queen at Netley.

At the beginning of the twentieth century, the church authorities deemed Holy Trinity in need of enlargement. In order to raise funds for a new chancel and vestry, a bazaar was held at Connaught Drill Hall in 1902. This, however, was no ordinary bazaar. The mother of Revd Arnold's sister-in-law, Mrs Tyler, had been a lady-in-waiting to Queen Victoria and, during her time in service, had become friendly with the Queen's youngest daughter, Princess Beatrice. The princess, the widow of Prince Henry of Battenberg, was invited to open the bazaar and, to the delight of local people, she accepted.

On the day of her visit, Fareham was *en fête*. Crowds greeted her at the railway station and cheered her en route to Connaught Drill Hall. She was welcomed by South Hampshire MP Arthur Lee, while the director of Fareham Philharmonic Society, Eugene Spinney, conducted a string orchestra. Bouquets were provided by Drover's Nurseries of Trinity Street, and local groups entertained the royal party with theatrical sketches. The success of the occasion provided the necessary funds and the church improvements were finally completed in 1913. Just eight years later Holy Trinity again received an important visitor, though this time the occasion was an altogether more sombre one, as the war memorial honouring the many fallen Fareham heroes was unveiled by Earl Haig.

The rapidly increasing population of Fareham, housed in new estates and developments around the edges of the town, resulted in the need for new churches by the early 1960s. The church of St Columba was opened in 1963 to serve worshippers from the Highlands Road area, while that of St John the Baptist was constructed to a dramatic design in St Michael's Grove for the inhabitants of the West End area. Around this time repairs were needed to Holy Trinity when it was discovered that the southeastern corner of the church was sinking and some stone was falling from the tower. Whilst work was done to try to rectify this situation, the interior was attractively redecorated in white and gold. The

In March 1992 work began on the demolition of Holy Trinity Church spire, which had become unsafe. Here scaffolding is in place ready for work to begin.

Towards the end of March 1992 half of the spire had been demolished.

church spire, however, continued to cause problems. After the 1987 gales and the fierce storms of 1990, a thorough inspection of the spire in 1991 suggested that it might not withstand further severe weather. 'The spire has been worn away by age and atmosphere,' said Revd Roy Kingston. The reluctant decision was taken in 1992 to demolish the spire. Fascinated shoppers watched the day-by-day dismantling of this Fareham landmark, 160ft above ground level. A temporary roof was placed over the tower and on Easter Sunday the mayor, Malcolm Harper, hoisted the flag of St George atop the new pole which had replaced the spire.

In the late 1980s a new church was built in Osborn Road South for the benefit of many local worshippers. The splendid United Reformed Church, opened in 1994, replaced the Grade II listed edifice which has stood so prominently in West Street since 1836. The new church, which cost £740,000 to build, has an illuminated cross on its 46ft high tower, while outside is the Diana, Princess of Wales memorial garden, completed in September 1998. There is a long history of dissenting worship in Fareham. During the 1670s, various groups which had taken issue with the established Church of England met at a house in the Old Rope Walk, Lower Quay. A new meeting-house was built, one of the preachers being Mr Chandler. He had another meeting-house built, upon which site was finally built the West Street church in 1836 at a cost of £1,000 and including some of the bricks from the previous structure. The church, together with the new Portland Buildings nearby, certainly enhanced this part of West Street. Over the years, the edifice became first the Congregational Church and finally the United Reformed Church. When the new church in Osborn Road South was built, it was decided that the old building should be preserved; as the new Market Quay development began, however, builders moved in to transform it into a restaurant-cum-wine bar. An extension was added, with tall slot windows to match the church. Thus one of West Street's finest old buildings lives on although, regrettably, the former Sunday school was demolished. One wonders what the stern dissenters who originally worshipped there would make of the typically twenty-first century utilisation of their building!

A long-time near neighbour of the old Congregational Church was the original Fareham Methodist Church, built in 1875 on a prominent site along West Street on the other side of Portland Street. This imposing structure saw many changes in its vicinity over the years; the Savoy Buildings, together with the cinema, appeared across the road, while peace was also disturbed by the erection of the Hants & Dorset bus station on its eastern side. Eventually the Methodists decided to build a brand new church in 1939 at the junction of King's Road and Queen's Road. In recent years the church has had a fine new hall built alongside. The interior is enhanced by fine stained-glass windows in memory of Messrs Dodge and Pyle, prominent local shopkeepers whose philanthropic works on behalf of the less fortunate in the town were well known. The original church in West Street, then disused, was finally demolished in the 1950s to make way for an entrance from Hartlands Road to the bus station, when it was extended westwards.

Yet another place of worship that had a change of venue was the Baptist Church. In the late-nineteenth

✤ SOME FAREHAM CHURCHES ✤

Holy Trinity Church in May 2005. Although the spire is long since gone, the church remains a reassuring and strong presence in the midst of the busy town.

The old St Columba's Church in Catisfield Lane in October 1983, long after the building had ceased to function as a place of worship. Somewhat distant from Holy Trinity and known as the 'Tin Tabernacle', it was built in 1891 to serve the people in the area.

A new St Columba's was built in 1961 to replace the 'Tin Tabernacle', seen here in a sad state of dereliction.

The former Congregational Church of 1836, unused as a place of worship since the 1990s, has been preserved within the new Market Quay development. In 2005 work began to convert the former church into a meeting place of a very different nature – a bar/restaurant!

November 2005, with the conversion of the Congregational Church complete, including the addition of the glass-walled extension. This is now the 'Vanguard' bar.

In September 1979 the old Congregational Church, latterly the United Reformed Church, was still in regular use in its rather incongruous setting near the Woolwich Building Society and the children's play area. The Woolwich moved into new premises in the Market Quay development and the building shown here is no more.

Fareham Methodist Church, May 2005. This church was built in 1939, replacing the former building on West Street which was finally demolished in the 1950s when the bus station was extended. The church was enhanced by the addition of the Welcome Centre to the frontage along Queens Road.

The entrance to the Garden of Reflection at the United Reformed Church, December 2005. This peaceful retreat, built as part of the scheme to commemorate the life of Diana, Princess of Wales, was completed in 1998.

SOME FAREHAM CHURCHES

Six girls ready to entertain at a Fareham Methodist Church junior concert in the early 1960s. From left to right: Patricia Day, Brenda Coffin, Barbara Jones, Rosina White, Pam Spencer, Penny Ward.

The United Reformed Church was built in 1994 in Osborn Road South. This picture, taken in December 2005, features the 46ft high tower with the cross on top.

century, the Baptists met in a church in West Street not far from the corner of Hartlands Road. After this was demolished in the early 1930s a new church was erected on the site of a former water-bottling plant along Gosport Road. In 1981, however, the plans for the widening of the A32 resulted in the need for this building to be removed. The money raised by Fareham churchgoers, together with a loan from the national Baptist church organisation and the compensation paid as a result of the compulsory purchase order, enabled a new church to arise beside the widened road. Opened in November 1981 with a dedication service led by Revd George Lindo, the hexagonal building, which has no windows on the side next to the road in order to combat traffic noise, has proved a very successful replacement. In more recent times, another Baptist church, Hill Park, has opened to serve worshippers in the Highlands Road and Gudge Heath areas.

Wholesale traffic changes, the development of the bus station and the demolition of many small houses and shops in the area just south of West Street have combined to leave the splendid Catholic Church of the Sacred Heart in a rather isolated position. Until 1878 Catholics had no church of their own in the town; in 1874, however, an Army chaplain, Father Thomas Foran, who lived in High Street, purchased a plot of land, once Sandy's timberyard, with a view to erecting a church there. With the help of the Grace and Stapleton-Bretherton families, enough money was raised to build the church, which was opened in September 1878 in the charge of the first priest, Father Gascoigne. With the appointment of Father Edward Collins in 1887, the church began to grow in popularity. The church hall, formerly the school-room, was developed in 1894. In 1978 Sacred Heart celebrated its centenary with a consecration and thanksgiving Mass held by Revd Anthony Emery, the Catholic Bishop of Portsmouth, at which 14 former priests of the parish were present. The fact that this particular church reached this milestone was in no small part due to a rescue operation undertaken by a group of sailors who were attending a social function in the church hall in 1941 when an incendiary bomb landed in the organ gallery during an enemy raid.

The Catholic Church of the Sacred Heart, built in 1878 on the site of a timber yard. Various road works and the demolition of buildings in this area have left this popular place of worship in rather striking solitude, as seen here in May 2005.

The King's Centre, December 2005. Next door to the former Techno Trade in West Street, it is home to Fareham Community Church. Members of this non-denominational church purchased this former furniture shop in 1996 and transformed it into a centre seating 250 people and with various other facilities for worshippers.

Today both Sacred Heart and its daughter church, St Philip Howard in Bishopfield Road – which, with its notable wood carvings by Norman Gaches, was opened in June 1980 – enjoy large attendances and provide much support to local and international charity projects.

Another religious organisation that has proved successful in the town is the Fareham Community Church. Founded in 1981, this non-denominational church at one time met in Fareham College. In the 1990s, however, its membership had increased considerably and the elders set their sights on giving the church a home of its own to provide a wider range of activities and to develop its outreach work. In 1996 the Community Church bought a former furniture shop in West Street and transformed it into a new centre with seating for 250 people, a coffee bar, activities room and a crèche, together with facilities for younger members. Today the King's Centre remains the home of this church, which plays a large part in serving the Fareham community through its principles of care, fellowship and faith.

The successful and vigorous life of Fareham's churches is a welcome contrast to today's often self-centred and secular society. Perhaps nowhere is this strength of religious feeling better shown than in the organisation of 'Churches Together in Fareham', within which all denominations have worked together to provide a focus for pastoral care and practical help within the community.

CHAPTER 5

Fareham's Lost Industries

Every community up and down the land has had its local trades and small industries. Fareham is no exception and can lay claim to several which extended beyond the town and were of national significance. The production of fine-quality leather through tanning was one such. Probably many of us today regard fine leather goods as luxury items. Leather gloves, shoes, handbags and travel cases are all quite expensive items and for many people cheaper substitutes are available in a variety of plastics. Things were very different in the past. One of the most interesting and enjoyable ways of understanding this is through a display at the *Mary Rose* Museum in Portsmouth Dockyard, where the unfortunate sailors' possessions and clothing, all made of leather, are exhibited. We can see leather jerkins, shoes, gloves and even buckets, essential on board ship for washing the decks as well as for fire fighting. In former centuries the horse, with or without a cart or wagon, was the single means of transport. The horse had to be saddled and bridled, while the carriage attachments and fittings were of leather – a natural material that is strong, supple and water-resistant. The importance, therefore, of the tanner's trade to our ancestors cannot be over-estimated.

Fareham's tanning industry dates back at least as far as the reign of Charles I. A Wiltshire family, the Rolfes, started the tannery at Wallington and by the end of the seventeenth century, when another Wiltshire family, the Threshers, joined it, the business was well established. Peter Thresher had married William Rolfe's daughter and both families became involved in the community life of rural Fareham. The Thresher and Rolfe male family members became part of its establishment, serving as church-wardens, magistrates and clergymen. From the nineteenth century, the Sharland family from Devon would be the last owners of this historic business. The incoming owners of the tannery embedded themselves so securely in the little community that was Fareham possibly because the men employed were all from local families. With sons following fathers into the trade perhaps the tannery owners were careful to create a fellow feeling of sharing the success and its rewards with these skilled workers, who were so essential to them.

Wallington was the ideal site for the tanning trade, being close to the quay from where the hides could easily be shipped out to all parts of the country. When the railways were established in the 1840s, even better and quicker transport could convey the goods to wider markets.

The process of tanning is at least 7,000 years old and was always quite labour intensive. The basis of the tanning liquid was a mixture of oak-bark and valencia nut, raw materials which were obtained from trees in the New Forest and the Forest of Bere. The oak bark was immersed in liquor pits, vats fashioned from large wooden boxes and sunk into the ground. At the tannery, the men prepared the skins by removing the rump, tail and burr of the animal; edible pieces were the worker's perks! Another group of men, the fleshers, scraped away the fat and tissue from the skins, which would previously have been steeped in lime pots for the easier removal of fat and hair. After numerous soakings in lime, the skins were immersed in the oak bark tanning pits. This odorous process took many months as the skins progressed through several pits with ever stronger tanning solutions.

The drying and rolling of the hides was the culmination of a very long procedure which was left in the hands of the most skilled tanners because only the smoothest, scratch-free leather could achieve the highest prices on the markets. Virtually nothing was wasted in the tanning process. The drained and dried oak bark was used as fuel for the home hearth and was also excellent for smoking hams from the many pigs reared in the backyards of labourers' cottages.

While this age-old industry ran on profitably for nearly three centuries, it had its drawbacks. The tanning liquid stained hands and faces and the smell of the soaking hides permeated the air in a way which today, certainly, would be environmentally unacceptable. The Sharland family sold the business in the early years of the last century and before the First World War it had ceased to function. There is

Workers at Wallington Tannery, c.1900.

Brickworkers in the 1930s. Huge numbers of bricks from Fontley were used in the construction of the Palmerston Forts between 1859 and 1870.

The Lower Swanwick Brickworks cricket team of 1908. Brickworkers were prominent in local sport for many years.

Tiles are being loaded into railway trucks at Fontley in the 1920s.

little or nothing to remind local people today of this once important Fareham industry.

It can be said with some justification that the Fareham brickmaking business reached far beyond Hampshire, the famous Fareham Reds being supplied all over the country. London's Royal Albert Hall was constructed with them, as was the old St Thomas's Hospital, opened by Queen Victoria in 1871. On the Isle of Wight, the Queen's beloved Osborne House was partly constructed of Reds, while at Cape Town in South Africa the burghers chose these famous bricks for the construction of their majestic town hall.

In the first half of the nineteenth century, the new railway system was of huge benefit to the brick industry, as it was to so many other concerns. In this particular instance, the building of culverts, tunnels and viaducts required millions of bricks. The apotheosis of Fareham's brick manufacturing past is

Bursledon Brickworks football team, c.1932.

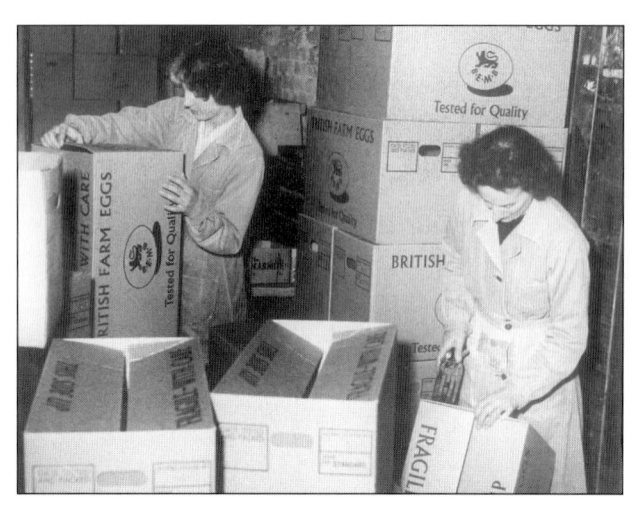

The Fareham Market Co. was founded in 1880 in a field behind West Street for the sale of stock, catering largely for the farms on the Delme estates, which extended from Privett to Curdridge. Over the years, the character of the market changed. In 1959, local girls are seen packing 'British Lion' eggs at the market.

The market in the mid-1970s. The site is the same, but the animals have long since disappeared and been replaced by clothing and general household stalls. Today this site has vanished beneath the new developments.

surely the magnificent Quay viaduct, an impressive piece of architecture which totally outshines its modern road counterpart. British foreign policy in the mid-nineteenth century gave another boost to the local brickmaking industry. Prime Minister Palmerston's decision to build a chain of sea and land ports as protection against possible invasion from France ensured full employment in local yards. The majority of the forts, known colloquially as the Palmerston Follies, are constructed from Fareham Reds. It is perhaps a tribute to both the quality of the raw material and the skill of the men that, even today, almost the entire range of forts is still *in situ* and they are rightly regarded as part of the built heritage of this country. Two of the largest brickmaking yards, at Fontley and Bursledon, survived well into the twentieth century; Bursledon, which closed in 1974, is now a much-enjoyed visitors' centre, displaying the skills of the building trade over the centuries.

Not only bricks came from these local yards, but also clay tiles, drainage pipes, garden pots, pots for storage purposes and, perhaps most renowned, chimney pots. Fareham once dominated the market in these vital and attractive building components. The leading name in the eighteenth- and nineteenth-century clay goods business was Thomas Stares, whose family company exported products throughout the South West region. It can be quite an enjoyable experience when on walks round parts of historic Hampshire to gaze up to the rooftops and pick out the Fareham pots adorning the roofs of buildings. There are many hundreds of them to be seen, distinctive because of their special shape. Typically they are approximately 4ft in height and taper from a width of about 4ft across the base to 9in. across the top. There is sometimes a piecrust-type extrusion and then below it one or two bands of white slip, sometimes in a wavy or geometric design. The chimney pots were made in two parts; because they were so tall it was impossible for the average-sized potter to reach the whole way down inside the pot. Before firing, the two halves had to be joined together while still damp. This was a tricky operation and distortions sometimes occurred. The result was a distinctive and rather attractive quality which today is much prized by collectors – if they can get their hands on them! In the last century, the best known potteries were at North Hill, where pots were produced until well after the Second World War. In the early days of BBC Television there was a reminder of Fareham's great industry in the 'interlude' or test card symbol of that time, which showed the hands of Charlie Carver, who lived in one of the potters' cottages and had spent his entire working life at North Hill.

Before leaving the brick industry, mention should be made of the many fine Georgian-fronted houses in High Street. A number of these were built using another distinctive local product, a handsome blue-grey brick, its colour the result of a charring and burning process applied to the original red clay. Eighteenth-century Fareham rapidly became the preferred place of residence of both the new gentry and retired Admirals. For the more muted elegance of their houses they chose this particular blue-grey brick. Portchester had its own small clay-based industry, although it had nothing to do with building. Smoking of the long clay pipes known as churchwardens, often seen in old paintings, became popular towards the end of the seventeenth century. As the price of tobacco fell, smoking became more widespread and a clay pipe industry began to flourish. It appears to have begun here in the early years of the nineteenth century and lasted for a little over 100 years. During this time the small industry was the preserve of two local families, the Russells and the Leighs. There is also evidence of another smaller works at the Old

CHAPTER 6

Sea and Quay

A century ago, the entry for Fareham in Murray's *Handbook for Travellers in Hampshire* drew attention to the town's considerable trade, explaining that vessels of as much as 300 tons burden could tie up at the quayside. Today, however, shipping and its associated trades have long since gone. Although there are pleasure boats and some marine engineering and supply firms, Lower Quay, now a conservation area, is outflanked by the almost unending flow of cars, lorries and vans along the road into Fareham, their occupants having only a fleeting moment to glance at the tranquil waterfront.

Before the advent of the motor vehicle, the waterside was an important part of the town's economic life. Vessels of all shapes and sizes negotiated a careful pathway from Portsmouth Harbour, through Fareham Lake opposite Cams Bay, then through Heavy Reach and the Salterns before tying up at the quay. Here such merchandise as coal, corn, salt and hides was exchanged for Fareham's timber, leather, pottery, bricks and whiting for clay pipes. In the twentieth century, however, a combination of the decline in Fareham's export industries, the development of road travel and the gradual silting up of large parts of the creek reduced the town's position as a trading port.

Besides trading, the quays were also used for shipbuilding. In earlier times, timber was brought in to the town from Fareham Park and Titchfield Park and local people used the considerable raw materials to build boats. An early record reveals that in October 1403, a ship named *Marie* was to be made ready at Fareham for King Henry IV. In 1535 James Hawkysworth wrote to Viscount Lisle, Sheriff of Hampshire, to inform him that:

> ... *your ship sailed from Fareham on Sunday 26th September. Have sent in her 7000 of Tayl wood and a great ox from the prior of Christchurch; anchor stocks with a piece of ash to make axles of; a hogshead of salt.*

A letter to the same sheriff three years later from Sir Antony Windsor informed him of the quality of timber in the area:

> *As to your great wood you wrote for, there is a thousand readily tallied in Farahame Park and a thousand more shall be ready shortly...*

In 1636 Fareham, as a port, was required to pay £50 'ship money', a tax introduced by Charles I to help

A nineteenth-century oil painting showing a regatta day at Fareham Creek. A train passes along the 1848 viaduct while a boat festooned with flags lies near the shore with a huge marquee prominent in the background.

This painting is called The Port of Fareham. *For many years, before the railway appeared and roads improved, water connections were a vital part of Fareham's market-town commercial activity.*

pay for the wars with France and Spain. To the same ends, two years later the town was ordered to provide a ship of 400 tons and a company of 160 men for the king's service. Such activity, together with Sir John Coke's recommendation to the king that Fareham, rather than Chatham, might be used as a naval harbour at this time, shows the contemporary importance of the town's waterfront.

Despite these advantages, Fareham was not destined to develop into a naval dockyard. There was some military activity here during the Napoleonic wars, when the deep-water channel from Portsmouth Harbour brought unwelcome visitors to the quays in the form of French prisoners of war. These men were transferred from their captured ships and put aboard dismal prison hulks at various points in and around the harbour, 18 of the hulks, containing at least 9,000 prisoners, being moored

The old Ropewalk building in Lower Quay Close. As well as being a rope manufactory, it also once housed sick and injured French prisoners during the Napoleonic Wars.

With the River Wallington prone to flooding around Broadcut and Wallington Shore Road, here work is in progress as part of the Council's Wallington Flood Alleviation Scheme in January 1983.

haphazardly in Fareham Lake. Many prisoners were allowed out for exercise on the quayside, where they were permitted to beg or to sell such items as bone combs for a penny or two to fascinated Fareham folk. Some locals feared the prisoners might bring disease into the town; this apprehension was considerably increased when a primitive hospital was set up at Lower Quay for injured and seriously ill prisoners. Those who died were buried in nearby Hospital Fields – a skeleton unearthed from the clay and gravel by workmen in 1963 was thought to be that of a French prisoner.

Many boats have been built at Fareham for both leisure and business. The Burrell and Fitchett family firms produced not only military vessels, including sloops, but also some larger trading boats. The local firms of Chippendale, See and Hamper continued the boat-building tradition. Percy See produced commercial, cruising and racing craft, including spectacular speedboats that had success in competitions throughout the world. The Hamper firm built yachts, doreys and lifeboats, besides other craft, at their Upper Wharf and Mill Lane yards for over half a century until 1986. Today, smaller firms provide facilities for the pleasure boat industry as well as marina moorings and lettings.

The very long stretch of water around the south-eastern edge of Fareham, all the way round from Wallington to Fleetlands, has provided many contrasts of scenery and land usage. For many years the wealthy residents in such grand houses as Cams, Northwood, Southfield and Elmhurst could enjoy their waterside views in a relaxed atmosphere; Dr Woakes of Belvoir House could walk across to the quayside from his home and fire up his impressive steam yacht for a leisurely sail along the creek. Intruding upon this tranquil scene, however, were more workaday buildings and concerns. The gasworks built in the 1860s, while providing a vital source of energy for the town, disfigured the coastal scene at Lower Bath Lane for over a century. At

The programme cover of the eight-day visit of the French fleet to the area in August 1905. The event was a huge publicity exercise to promote the supposed entente cordiale *between Britain and France.*

Lower Quay, industrial buildings such as the 1897 electricity generating station, the imposing former Fareham Steam Flour Mill and the sewage works at Salterns contrast with the yellow-brick Prospect House and the little group of eighteenth-century cottages in the Mill Yard area.

In the nineteenth and twentieth centuries, swimmers, now largely confined to the safer waters of indoor pools, were a frequent sight in the creek.

✣ SEA AND QUAY ✣

The visiting French sailors at Portchester, being treated to a sit-down tea, 1905.

Cams Mill, built on the site of an earlier mill, mentioned in the Domesday Book.

The quayside, designated a conservation area by Fareham Council in the 1970s. Here, in June 1982, work is in progress to improve the promenade at Town Quay.

A view of Town Quay in 1979, with the main Gosport road on the left.

SEA AND QUAY

A view from the early 1980s, taken from Lower Quay. In the second half of the twentieth century, pleasure boats took the place of commercial vessels.

During the 1930s the urban district of Fareham was enlarged as a result of the acquisition of rural parishes, including the village of Warsash. This boating and residential hamlet provided Fareham with a waterfront along the east bank of the River Hamble. The little ferry that links Warsash with Hamble is seen here in 1948, at the bottom of Shore Road.

A 1950s view of Bath Lane, near the creek and the recreation ground. Note the lifebelt placed strategically on a nearby wall!

The popular waterfront pub, the Rising Sun, at Warsash.

Tucked away from the busy main road into Fareham, The Castle In The Air pub, pictured here in 1987, presents an attractive place for refreshment for visitors to the quayside.

Cams Hall had its own private bathing house at one time, at the bay end of an avenue of oaks and elms known as Bathing House Grove. In 1836 a group of Fareham businessmen financed the building of a seawater bathing house in the upper reach of the creek. So popular did this new amenity become that the road by which it was situated, then known as Park Lane, was renamed Bathing House Lane and later Bath Lane. Swimmers also enjoyed taking to the waters round the town quays, as well as in the old Mill Pond. Cams Mill, a once picturesque sight sketched and painted by many artists, including the celebrated local painter Martin Snape, was pulled down in 1920, while the Mill Pond itself, together with Cams Quay, disappeared beneath the huge road developments of the 1960s which produced the Delme Arms roundabout. This historic area of Fareham might have been preserved if the ideas of local councillor Charles Senior had been taken up in the 1920s. He proposed that the water could be dammed at Bridgefoot, where the River Wallington joined Fareham Creek, thus turning the northern end of the creek into a lake. Senior envisaged the creation of boating facilities on the lake, which could be surrounded by pleasure gardens and walks. The idea was not taken up, although in the 1930s similar schemes were suggested.

Eventually apathy set in and the mill pond silted up, often giving off an unpleasant smell, besides becoming the depository for various unwanted items of household rubbish. Today virtually the only memory of the once-popular Mill Pond is a plaque on the railway viaduct recording its former presence.

Gradually, the attraction of swimming elsewhere in the creek began to fade. Whether people today are more worried about hygiene and pollution than their forbears is a matter for conjecture, but certainly the dumping of German submarines, captured in the First World War and dismantled in the creek in the early 1920s, produced quite serious fuel spillages into the waters, to the detriment of fishermen and would-be swimmers alike. Meanwhile, as attention after the Second World War began to turn towards town centre development and the provision of road alterations to cope with increasing traffic, the waterfront went into a slow decline. The creek gradually silted up, businesses closed and by 1970 Town Quay began to assume a rather forlorn appearance. The old sewage works at Salterns was deemed inadequate to serve the evolving town, but before rebuilding and enhancements could take place there were complaints about the smell from the creek. In 1973 over 100 public-spirited individuals combined in a scheme to try to clean up the waterside. Dismal and squalid heaps of rubbish, including old bicycles, exhaust pipes and tyres, were retrieved from the water. Despite wearing protective gloves, a local doctor helping with the rubbish retrieval suffered a

A fine character study from 1902 of the crew and friends aboard the Dorris *in Fareham Creek.*

cut which became seriously infected through unpleasant organisms caused by discharged sewage. In 1974 a local fisherman reported the awful sight of dying crabs and eels climbing over each other in a desperate attempt to escape the polluted waters.

Improvements to the sewerage system gradually took effect and the creek became cleaner. In 1980 the sewage was finally diverted to the Peel Common works, leaving the Salterns outflow to cope with storm waters only. In August 1989, however, the main pipe carrying sewage from Salterns to Peel Common fractured, causing a grim discharge of effluent into some streets. Later in the same year, while a new main pipe was being connected into the system, more sewage waste water appeared in the creek, although it had been screened and passed through effluent tanks before discharge. Since then, however, the water has improved in quality and there has been considerable increase in the wildlife supported by the creek.

Today the quayside is a designated conservation area. The council has improved the walkway, providing seats at certain spots along the waterside where one can turn one's back on the noisy traffic and gaze out at a much more tranquil scene across the creek. The Fareham Society, instrumental in so many areas with regard to both the maintenance of the town's heritage and the raising of environmental issues, has promoted the quay area in a detailed booklet describing the interesting sights to be seen on a walk from Bath Lane to the Public Hard at Lower Quay. Steeped in history and standing in sharp contrast to the modern shopping centre, the Fareham waterside is an asset to the town.

✦ CHAPTER 7 ✦

Titchfield and the Earls of Southampton

These houses in South Street date from the fifteenth century. The term 'eavesdropping' derives from the way in which the first floors of this type of construction project out over the ground floor.

The word 'village' hardly does justice to today's Titchfield. Admired and loved by residents and visitors alike, it has a rich history and its buildings include some of the finest in Hampshire. Yet among all the business and commercial developments at Sarisbury, Whiteley and Locks Heath, the heart of Titchfield remains virtually unscathed by any intrusive modern developments. Walking through the Square today, it is still possible to envisage the bustle of village life in the eighteenth and nineteenth centuries. The Bugle inn and the Queen's Head remind us of the coaching trade passing through to take villagers out and beyond the Square to Winchester, Southampton, even London. The area outside the Bugle was for centuries the site of the village stocks, where miscreants were chained and at the mercy of their abusive neighbours. On a happier note, the Square's small businesses and traders offered a wide variety of services to local people. Linen drapers, dressmakers and boot and shoemakers sat cheek by jowl with saddlers, grocers, butchers and attorneys. The oldest industry in the village was the tannery, dating from the medieval period and still functioning in the 1950s, ideally situated close to the River Meon. As with the Wallington tannery at Fareham, the trade provided employment for many Titchfield families at a time when leather as a commodity was widely used, before the introduction of plastic substitutes in the twentieth century. The tanning trade is remembered today in a southern area, close to the churchyard, called Skinhouse Piece.

Domesday Titchfield had the name of Ticefel and, in the time of William the Conqueror, was almost

A house in Church Street, Titchfield, in 1987. Like many others in the village, it is of medieval origin.

53

Schoolchildren and their teachers eagerly await the arrival of a procession in Titchfield Square in 1935 during the celebration of the silver jubilee of King George V.

Titchfield celebrates the coronation in 1937 of King George VI. Flags festoon the large stores of Lankester & Crook, while the banner stretched across the street in the distance expresses the hope 'Long May He Reign'.

A drawing by B.J. Robertson showing St Peter's Church. Originally a Saxon church, many additions and changes have taken place to the building over the centuries. The spire, which to some may seem somewhat heavy for the tower it sits on, was added in the seventeenth century.

St Peter's Church before the controversial new vestry was built in the 1980s. As a result of the changes, the Hornby window is no longer fully visible.

West Hill Park School, October 1981, formerly a fine manor house dating from the eighteenth century.

wholly engaged in various types of farming. The Domesday Book records land for ploughing, woodlands, meadows and mills. The Bishop of Winchester held much of the land scattered around the centre of the village, as did assorted earls and counts. From 1086 until the early-twentieth century there were at least six mills operating on the River Meon, grinding the corn from these fertile meadows.

The ancient church of St Peter dates from the earlier Anglo-Saxon period. Its layers of history can easily be picked out in the flint, brick and stonework on the exterior of the church. A magnificent Norman doorway, with its characteristic rounded and richly decorated arch, leads into the north aisle, where the tall, slender columns date from the fifteenth century, as does the attractive conical tower.

The church suffered during the Reformation, as did so many others up and down the land, when its colourful murals were whitewashed over and the ancient stained glass smashed. Victorian restoration of the church proved controversial when the galleries were removed, together with the old box pews. The Norman south aisle reappeared in the Decorated style beloved of the mid-Victorian period. In the 1980s another controversy raged over the proposed construction of new chapter rooms inside the fabric of the old church. In the end the incumbent vicar won the argument for modern community facilities against the conservationists' desire to preserve the integrity of the ancient building.

In and around the village there are a number of houses of unusual interest. St Margaret's Priory, which is of Tudor origin, has links with both the Wriothesley and Delme families. Its brick tower may even have provided a good lookout point for the expected Armada coming in from the Solent. In more recent centuries it could have served as an observation tower from which the owner could keep an eye on his workers, or perhaps enjoy the spectacle of the huntsmen and their hounds in full cry.

Titchfield's Market Hall formerly stood at the

A view of Place House, Titchfield, from the 1950s.

An attractive line drawing of the entrance to Place House, which is now under the protection of English Heritage.

centre of the Square on the corner of West Street. Erected early in the seventeenth century at the instigation of the third Earl of Southampton, it comprised a ground floor with an open arcade where local traders could lay out their wares for the delectation of the villagers. The upper floor was a large meeting place for all types of public events. Early prints show this as a handsome timber building interspersed with the herringbone pattern of bricks much favoured by the Elizabethans. By the middle of the twentieth century the Market Hall was in a dangerous state, the eventual solution for its salvation being to transfer it to the newly created Weald and Downland Museum in West Sussex. In 1971 the hall was carefully dismantled and re-erected in the museum, where today it remains one of the highlights of the collection of local vernacular buildings. Although the hall is no longer in the village, visitors to the Weald and Downland Museum can appreciate the age and architecture of this priceless piece of Titchfield's past.

Without question, two of Titchfield's architectural glories are Place House (the Abbey) and its Great Barn. Titchfield Abbey was founded in 1232 by the Bishop of Winchester, Peter des Roches. Of the order of the Premonstratensians, a French monastic order, the canons were required to regularly read spiritual matter, including devotional works, and to prepare and write such works. The vast number of books collected and indexed were the work of these Premonstratensians at Titchfield, the catalogue listing over 300 volumes for a readership of about 14 canons. Individual works, however, number over 1,000, all of which were separately catalogued. This unique piece of monastic scholarship is now in the Portland Collection on loan to the British Museum. There is also evidence to suggest that the collection was a lending library available to wealthy men who might have an interest in theology, logic and philosophy, always provided they could read Latin.

This centre of learning was violently swept away during the Dissolution of the Monasteries. Henry VIII, angry with the Church because of its opposition to his divorce of Catherine of Aragon and also eager while 16 girls were the responsibility of Miss Jane Bailey. Just 12 years later the numbers had risen to 347 infants and girls. Monitors, or in this case monitresses, were still being employed. Fanny Bishop was appointed monitress in 1880 at the age of 14 and was paid 3s. a week.

It would be perfectly possible to write a separate book sourced from the log-books of these early schools. For anyone interested in the occupations of the parents of Fareham's Victorian children, these books are a mine of information. We read that, in 1877, dozens of fathers were employed as bricklayers, tanners and potters, all reflecting the local economy of the period. A tinman, a sea captain and an asylum attendant are also listed. This last person may have worked at Knowle Hospital, which opened in 1852. Parents were required to pay 2d. a week for each child. To raise even this small sum was difficult for poor and often large families. Like many other small towns, Fareham had plenty of employment available in the traditional trades, but these were generally poorly paid and many jobs, such as strawberry-picking, were strictly seasonal.

Teachers as well as parents were faced with money problems. It was not the parents' humble weekly payments that were the main source of income but the capitation grant paid to head teachers, based on the results of testing the three Rs by itinerant government school inspectors. If the teaching was declared below standard and school attendance figures fell, the government grant was reduced. After 1880, when school attendance became compulsory, the head teachers' concern is reflected in the school log-books; because of sickness, bad weather or the pupils' lack of adequate footwear, teachers were despairing. Happily, not all was gloom and doom. One surprising feature of Victorian school life was the number of holidays enjoyed by staff and children. There would be regular half holidays to celebrate the innumerable royal births, marriages and deaths – Victoria had nine children and dozens of grandchildren. Frequent sports at Bath Lane recreation ground were much enjoyed, as was dancing around the maypole, an opportunity to dress in one's Sunday best. Fareham's Annual Regatta was a delight freely available to the poorest children and their families.

Long before the National Schools were established, Fareham had had many other types of fee-paying establishments. The earliest recorded school in Fareham is Mrs Bradley's ladies' boarding school in 1792. One well-regarded boys' school was Blenheim House, an old-established institution belonging to a Mr Grace and in existence from around 1855. Located at No. 14 West Street, in a directory of 1875 it is described as a boarding school for young gentlemen. Its headmaster from 1864, Harry Joseph Atkins, married Sarah Adams Dallimore in 1869, the latter being very much involved in the day-to-day management of the school, despite having ten children of her own. Atkins made sure that the school remained a family affair; one of his daughters married Alexander Baylis, who joined Blenheim House in 1889.

By examining the census figures over the period 1871–81, it can be seen that the number of pupils rose from 16 to 54. Atkins liked to keep the boys active and on the move. He arranged paper chases around Fareham and beyond, taking in Hill Head, Chark, Rowner and Lee-on-the-Solent. The rigorous regime included cricket, football and sailing in Atkins's own boat, the gig *Dolphin*, a tender rescued from an old man-o'-war. The lighter side of school life included a grand bonfire and fireworks on 5 November and summer outings organised by the redoubtable Mrs Atkins. When Atkins retired in December 1892, he became a freemason and was a founder-member of Fareham Rotary Club.

By 1901 Blenheim House had become a coeducational establishment. Its dormitories are described as large and airy and fitted throughout with electric lights. The headmaster, Mr R. Arnold, promised all home comforts at a rate of ten guineas a term.

In the second half of the nineteenth century, the

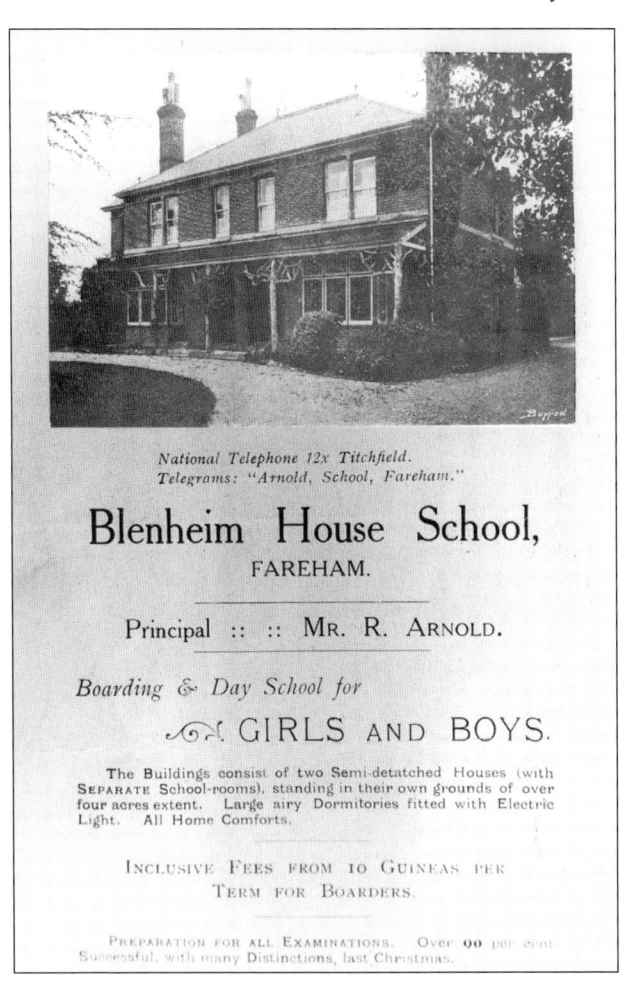

An advertisement for Mr Arnold's Blenheim House School, 1901. This co-educational establishment operated in two semi-detached houses to the north of West Street.

Milston High School – a grand title for a small establishment – in 1908. This little school, run by Miss Treadwell at No. 153 West Street, offered a modern curriculum including shorthand and typewriting.

The older buildings of Price's College in June 1989, shortly before demolition began.

numbers of small private schools had mushroomed. It has to be said, however, that many of these had an overwhelmingly Dickensian feel. A Miss Alston managed to squeeze 11 children between the ages of five and twelve into a classroom measuring 12ft by 15ft, furnished with just two desks and forms. Even more alarming were Mrs Kempster's 22 children, the youngest just one year old, all crammed into one room, while Mrs Ridlett managed somehow to fit 30 children into a room just 12ft square.

George Ashton (third from the right, second row), a popular headmaster of Price's College, with other members of staff on the occasion of his retirement in 1959.

✤ EDUCATION AND CHILDREN ✤

The official opening of Fareham Girls' Grammar School, 18 July 1957. Left to right: Miss M.E. Lowe, headmistress; Dr L. Scott-Fleming, the Bishop of Portsmouth, and Miss Rosemary Hilyard, art and geography teacher.

Miss Mary Rush with first-year girls in a botany class.

At the end of the nineteenth century Catisfield had its own small educational establishment, Broderick House, whose entrance gates proudly proclaimed it as a school for young gentlemen. It closed down in 1916. What might be described as its 'feeder' school was St Fillans in Southampton Road, run by the Misses Porter. Miss Jessie Porter was in charge, assisted by her three sisters, one of whom, Miss Norah, was once described as 'a real old dragon'!

Rather more upmarket were four girls' schools. These were the Misses Turner's establishment in Hartland Road, Miss Kiln's in Portland Street, Miss Blake's in Gosport Road and Miss Treadwell's in West Street, where the curriculum looked to the twentieth century and the modern woman. Her 'moderate' terms provided physical exercises and Swedish drill, for which a Sergeant Sampson was imported, while Madam Dunn came over from Southsea to instruct the older girls in the more traditional female accomplishments of dressmaking and needlework. Shorthand and typewriting were also

Second-year girls of Fareham Girls' Grammar, 1956.

63

A dress rehearsal of a production of The Snow Queen *by Fareham Girls' Grammar School in 1958.*

taught, preparing pupils for the better-paid skilled clerical work increasingly available to young women.

Far and away the best known and most prestigious of Fareham's many schools was Price's, the gift of William Price, a wealthy and philanthropic timber merchant whose 1721 will bequeathed his house in West Street, his estate at Crockers Hill and his farmlands at Elson, Gosport, to the minister and churchwardens of the parish of Fareham. These became the trustees charged with establishing a charity school for 30 poor children in the Price family home in West Street. The school was soon a flourishing concern, supported by an annual allowance of 40s. per pupil 'for the purchase of books and sea coals for firing.' Clearly Price was an affluent businessman. His will additionally decreed that the surplus from the rents on his properties be distributed among poor widows in the parish. The headmaster's salary in 1721 was £35 per annum plus free accommodation in the schoolhouse; 100 years later it rose to £52. An interesting comparison can be made with Jane Bailey's remuneration as head of the Fareham Board School for Girls in Wickham Road. In 1877 her pay was £100 per annum; she had responsibility for 200 pupils but no rent allowance.

Price's charity schoolchildren must have been quite noticeable in the mid-eighteenth rural parish that was Fareham. They wore smart blue cloaks over their uniforms of matching blue and their hats and shoes gleamed with silver buttons and buckles. The annual entrance examination, held on Ash Wednesday, was a simple affair, entrants being required only to read a passage from the Bible or prayerbook to the satisfaction of the vicar and

Part of the Wykeham House School photograph of 1949. Staff here include the headmistress, Miss G.A. Beer, Miss V. Jewell, Miss M. Cork, Miss E. Morris, Mrs M. Burman, Miss K. Pond, Miss Cocks and Miss M. Buckler. The only male member of staff is Mr E. Blomfield (third from right) *who taught Latin.*

✤ EDUCATION AND CHILDREN ✤

Pupils at Western House School in West Street pose on the doorsteps and at the windows in the early 1920s.

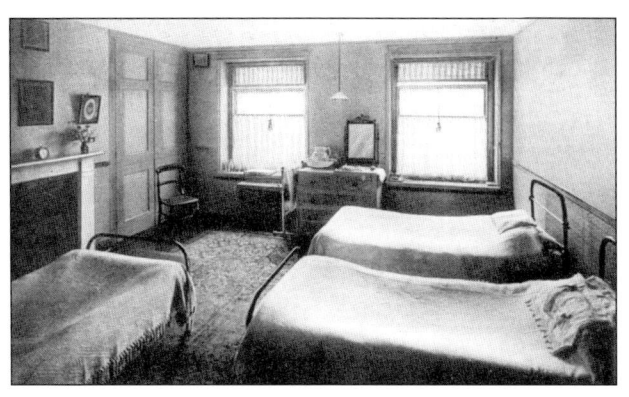

A dormitory in Western House School, 1925.

A game of lawn tennis in full swing in the grounds of Western House in 1925.

churchwardens. By 1846 Price's had ceased to be co-educational, and William Price's now dilapidated house in West Street was demolished and a new schoolhouse built in its place.

Until Fareham Grammar School opened in the 1950s, secondary education for girls was provided at Wykeham House School, which began life as Orme Lodge at No. 17 West Street. On 26 May 1916 the *Hampshire Telegraph* advertised it as a day and boarding-school for girls:

The aim of the school is to give a sound, modern education and special care is taken in the thorough grounding of the younger girls. Girls can be prepared for the Oxford and Cambridge Local Examination and for the Associated Board of the Royal Academy and Royal College of Music. Special classes for shorthand and typewriting and for elocution. Moderate and inclusive fees.

The advertisement was submitted by the headmistress, Alice Baylis, the eldest daughter of Henry Joseph Atkins of Blenheim House.

As the numbers of pupils increased, Alice Baylis moved the school to larger premises in Western House at No. 37 West Street. A further move took place in 1928 to the even more spacious Georgian splendour of No. 69 High Street. With this move came the new name of Wykeham House. It now, of course, occupies Fareham House in East Street. Former pupils recall the morning assemblies held in the beautiful conservatory-cum-garden, known as the music room, at No. 69 High Street. Fruit and vegetables from the high-walled garden were on the menu for wartime school dinners. The perhaps now rather unfashionable author of the Chalet School books for girls, Elinor Brent-Dyer, was a teacher during the Western House phase.

One of the most famous naval preparatory schools in England, Stubbington House was founded in 1841 by the Revd William Foster, vicar of Crofton, in the eighteenth-century manor house of Stubbington. It seems that the naval connection stemmed from the Revd Foster's wife, a daughter of Admiral John Haye. There is quite a sumptuous feel to the early curriculum. Senior pupils were supplied with wine and ale as an accompaniment to a regime of chemistry, music, fencing, gymnastics and rifle-shooting. The list of old boys is like a roll-call of British history, with an array of dukes and marquesses. Admiral Lord Charles Beresford, First Lord of the Admiralty and Member of Parliament for Portsmouth in the early years of the twentieth century was an alumnus, as was Queen Victoria's grandson, Alexander Battenberg, later the Marquess of Carisbrooke. The artist Sir John Millais sent his eldest son there, while another pupil was the wonderfully named Brudenell Hunt-Grubbe! Two old boys stand out from their illustrious predecessors, reflecting as they do the particular ethos of South Hampshire, with its long history of seafaring

65

Boys from Stubbington House, ready for a games period.

and aviation. They are Sir Robert Falcon Scott, of the doomed Antarctic expedition, and Sir Thomas Octave Murdoch Sopwith, yachtsman and aircraft designer.

During the Second World War, the school was evacuated to Cornwall. On its return to Stubbington, a Ministry of Education report of 1954 cast a critical eye over the school and its curriculum:

Although strong in academic subjects, art and the constructive crafts play only a minor role. The aesthetic side of education receives rather less than its due... it should be possible to broaden the curriculum and add more variety and enjoyment to life outside the classroom without damaging the boys' chances in the Common Entrance examination. However, on the whole, a good school.

By the late 1960s, the school had moved to its present location at Earlywood, Berkshire.

The story of Fareham's schools would not be complete without mentioning two which were outside what might be called mainstream education. At the Wallington–Delme junction, the Roundabout Hotel, a familiar landmark, had quite a different role nearly 150 years ago. Founded in 1869 by Lady Larcom, the wife of the Rt Hon. Sir Thomas Askew Larcom of Heathfield House, Titchfield Road, it was the Fareham Industrial Home for Girls aged 12–14 Years. This was transferred, 15 years later, to the Church of England Society for Providing Homes for Waifs and Strays under the auspices of the Archbishop of Canterbury and the Bishop of Winchester. It was, in effect, a charitable school for training destitute young girls in cookery, laundry work and general housewifery. The main subscribers were advised that they could take these girls as they wished, to work in their own houses. In 1907 the

The Fareham Industrial Home in 1889, when there were at least 30 girls living there.

Fareham Industrial Home, rebuilt as St Edith's Home for Girls, was operational until the late 1950s.

The second establishment in Fareham which was a special school of its kind was Florence White's School of English Cookery, opened in the 1930s at No. 160 West Street. Florence White came from the family which, for many years, had managed the Red Lion Hotel at Fareham. Her ideas of what constituted good English cooking may be judged from her book *Where Shall We Eat?*, published in 1935:

A roast pheasant with celery sauce... The correct way to make Lancashire Hotpot with Oyster... jugging of hare with redcurrant jelly... the making and frying of sausages... the frying of fish at which our girls and women who live on the coast excel.

Were these recipes, one wonders, cooked at the Red Lion? The cookery school was advertised nationally and regularly appeared in the *Good Food Registers* of

❖ EDUCATION AND CHILDREN ❖

St Edith's Home for Girls in the 1930s, with the River Wallington in the foreground.

Fareham Industrial Home,
(In connection with the Church of England Central Society for Providing Homes for Waifs and Strays.)

President :—HIS GRACE THE LORD ARCHBISHOP OF CANTERBURY.
Vice President :—THE LORD BISHOP OF WINCHESTER.

Secretary :—E. DE M. RUDOLF, Esq., Church House, Dean's yard, London.
Honorary Local Secretary :—EDGAR GOBLE, Esq.
Hon. Correspondent :—MISS GITTENS.
Hon. Treasurer :—COLONEL POWYS. Hon. Medical Attendant :—W. F. BROOK, Esq.
Matron :—MISS LETCH.

ON November 5th, one of the girls developed a rash which Mr. BROOK pronounced to be that of scarlet fever. Within a few hours she was removed to a cottage where she still remains cut off from all communication with the Home. The disease fortunately was of a very mild type. The house was fumigated; and most thankful are we to say that no other child has exhibited the least symptom of the disorder; and all are now in perfect health. Most grateful thanks are due to Mr. BROOK for his promptitude and kindness throughout.

On November 15th, Commander Scott WILLCOX, kindly gave a Lecture and Entertainment at the Town Hall, in aid of the Funds. After defraying the necessary expenses, a balance of £2 10 was handed in.

On the 25th, Major-General THORNTON invited all the children to tea, at his residence, which they very much enjoyed.

The Committee have gratefully to acknowledge the valuable gift of a Piano, from Mrs. MORGAN; an acquisition which has long been desired.

The following Gifts are also gratefully acknowledged:
Christmas gift of Sheets and Clothing—Mrs LONG, Downend; *Rabbits*—S. R. DELME, Esq., Cams Hall; *Clothing*—Mrs. A. PERCIVAL, Minster Close, Peterboro'; Miss WRAY, Holyrood, Rugby, (for special girl); The Chislehurst Dorcas Club, per Miss G. M. PLUMMER, Oak Lodge; Materials for cotton frocks from Mrs. Arthur POLE, Phantassie, Prestonkirk, N.B., and most kindly made up by her servant, E. MONTAGUE; *Apples*—Mrs. EDNEY, Fareham; *Parcel of Magazines*—Mrs. BUTLER, Fareham.

Extract from the Fareham Industrial Home minutes for November 1893, in which Mr Brook is commended for his prompt treatment of a case of scarlet fever. Note the names of kind benefactors, both local and national.

Fareham Industrial Home,
(In connection with the Church of England Central Society for Providing Homes for Waifs and Strays.)

President :—HIS GRACE THE LORD ARCHBISHOP OF CANTERBURY.
Vice President :—THE LORD BISHOP OF WINCHESTER.

Secretary :—E. DE M. RUDOLF, Esq., Church House, Dean's yard, London.
Honorary Local Secretary :—EDGAR GOBLE, Esq.
Hon. Correspondent :—MISS GITTENS.
Hon. Treasurer :—COLONEL POWYS. Hon. Medical Attendant :—W. F. BROOK, Esq.
Matron :—MISS LETCH.

AN Examination was held on the 15th ultimo, by the Rev. Mr. WISEMAN, Diocesan Inspector. His official report has not yet come to hand, but at the time he expressed himself very pleased with the general appearance and intelligence of the children.

Through the liberality of many friends the children have again enjoyed a very happy Christmas time.

The following Gifts are most gratefully acknowledged:
Rabbits—S. R. DELME, Esq. 'Xmas Beef—E. PADDON, Esq. Puddings, Mincepies, Meat, Fruit, Cakes, Sweets, &c.—Mrs. DEANE; Miss GORE-CURRIE; Mrs. THORNTON; Mrs. LONG; Mrs. TOWNSEND; Mrs. GATER; Mrs. BOND; Mrs. FROST; Mrs. BROOK; Mrs. GOBLE; Mrs. PHILLIPS; Mrs. MITTELL; and Mrs. PLATT. Christmas Cards & Crackers—Mrs. WAY, Bournemouth; Mrs. TOWNSEND; and Miss MILBURNE, Willesden. Blankets and Curtains—Mrs. LONG, Down End. Clothing—"A Friend"; Miss A. LLOYD, Bath; Miss GRESLEY's Work Party, Lichfield; Mrs. BROOK; Mrs. DRAYSON; Misses WRAY, Leamington, (for special girl); Mrs. STRONG's Bible Class, Peterborough; Miss LORD's Work Party, Sutton; Pupils of High School, Stoke Newington; Miss TILLEY, 73, S. George's Square, (for special girl); Mrs. CAMPBELL, Guernsey, (for special girl); Miss BADDELEY's Work Party, Cheltenham, (for special girl), and Miss SMALLMAN, Nuneaton, (for special girl).

Minutes from the Fareham Industrial Home, December 1893. Even more gifts have been donated at this Christmas time, Seymour Delme, it will be noted, having sent rabbits both this month and the last, possibly from a cull on his estate.

the 1930s, today's equivalent of the Michelin *Guides*. Florence White was a most unusual and versatile woman, who paved the way for the likes of Delia Smith and Nigella Lawson. Born in 1863, throughout her long life she held numerous jobs including governess, shopkeeper, newspaper reporter, fashion editor, social worker, even artist's model. Shortly before the Second World War, falling numbers at the school and Florence White's own poor health forced its closure. She died on 12 March 1940 at the former Fareham Workhouse in Wickham Road.

Fareham railway station, c.1910. The island platform where the train is waiting was added in 1889 when the direct Southampton route via Netley reached the town. At this time there were cattle pens behind the stored carriages to the left of the picture.

A Class 33 diesel locomotive with a rake of four coaches calling at Fareham with a Bristol–Portsmouth Harbour service in the mid-1980s.

CHAPTER 9

Railway Delights and Road Disasters

Just 200 years ago, Fareham residents rarely ventured further afield than to the town itself for their daily needs. Travel to distant places, when necessary, was neither comfortable nor convenient. Horse-drawn coaches could convey passengers to distant parts, but were expensive, slow and dangerous. Goods moved slowly, transported in heavy wagons along poor roads, while such inns as the Red Lion could provide post-chaises or small gigs, together with horses or drivers for hire, particularly for local travel. Slow improvements were effected to the roads out of town when the turnpike trusts were set up; this, however, was a somewhat erratic system whereby vehicles and riders coming in and out of town had to stop at closed gates to pay tolls, the monies thereby collected being used to maintain the roads, on the principle that those who used the roads should pay for them. Fareham's eastern and western approaches by road were guarded by gates and toll-houses erected by the Titchfield and Cosham Turnpike Trust, which operated six such entrances and exits in the area. The western toll-house and gate was at Blackbrook, and stood at the junction of Gudge Heath Lane and Redlands Lane with the main Titchfield Road. To the east, the turnpike which controlled the road to Portchester at its junction with Downend Road was known as the East Cams toll-gate, from the nearby farm of that name. Travellers from the north into Fareham via the Wickham Road had to pay their dues at Old Turnpike, although before the steeper section of Wickham Road was built the turnpike was situated at North Hill. Early maps do not show a toll-gate immediately to the south of the town, but it is known that there was a turnpike at Brockhurst on the road into Gosport.

The trusts and the task of road maintenance were gradually taken over during the second half of the nineteenth century by the newly empowered local authorities. By this time, a quite revolutionary new form of transport, the railway, had come into being. In mid-Victorian Britain, the rapid growth of railway networks brought opportunities for travel and distribution of goods at a speed and economy unimaginable to any citizen at the beginning of the century. Fareham's first railway link arrived in 1841, in the form of a branch line almost 16 miles long off the main Southampton to London line at Bishopstoke (now Eastleigh) by way of Botley, through the town and on to Gosport.

We can only imagine the interest and fascination that this new venture would have brought to local people as construction work proceeded southwards. Thomas Brassey, the contractor, imagined that the building of the new line would be a relatively easy project, but one tunnel proved a serious problem. About 600 yards in length, this tunnel burrowed beneath a ridge in the landscape with its southern portal near what is now the junction of Highlands Road and Miller Drive. It had proved difficult to construct, owing to the peculiarities of the type of clay encountered, which was particularly slimy and unstable when wet. Less than a month before the planned opening of the line, a serious slip occurred inside the tunnel, followed later by a partial collapse. Brassey decided to replace part of the tunnel with a cutting in order to ensure stability – that is why there are, in effect, two tunnels here today, with a short opening between them – and at last the line was completed. Meanwhile, Fareham's first railway station was being built, the line proceeding to Gosport over an elegant bridge across the Titchfield Road. Early prints suggest that the original station was somewhat different from the one we see today, although the approach road was similar and the Railway Hotel – where, in 2006, the Prague Junction nightclub stands – was added not long after the line was completed. On Monday 7 February 1842 the first ever train seen in Fareham arrived from London en route to Gosport. Its arrival was witnessed by large crowds, many excited and optimistic, others apprehensive. Soon a regular service of up to nine trains a day to London, together with local services to Southampton via Bishopstoke, was in place.

The fastest London trains, which in those days terminated at Nine Elms, took just under three hours to complete the journey. The trip to Gosport, offering local travellers unfamiliar views of their own town as the line crossed Mill Lane and Newgate Lane, took about 20 minutes.

The fact that the first line into Fareham continued to Gosport explains why the station was sited somewhat away from the main part of the town. It might have been situated more centrally if the Portsmouth extension had been built first, but this line was not constructed until 1848. As it was, the siting of the station at the extreme end of West Street had the effect, in the latter half of the century, of extending Fareham with the building of new houses, business premises and some shops. When the Portsmouth line was constructed, however, Fareham's landscape was changed forever. The new railway was built along an

Diesel-electric multiple units were used for many years on local services through Fareham before the lines were electrified. Here, in 1986, a train leaves Fareham on the curved line towards Portsmouth. The former lines to Gosport ran straight ahead.

Fareham station on May 6, 1990, Network South-East's Gala Day held to celebrate the completion of the electrification of local area services. Special shuttle trains, such as this electric multiple unit, were run all day with low fares to enable passengers to try the new service, which included the new station at Hedge End. The day ended with a fine fireworks display at Fareham station. In the foreground is a display demonstrating how the electrified rail was added to the existing lines.

RAILWAY DELIGHTS AND ROAD DISASTERS

A view of the station entrance c.1981. Since then the entrance has been smartened up and the former goods shed (on the right) demolished.

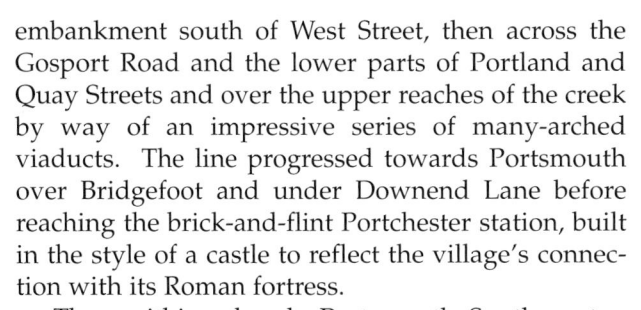

Members of the Fareham Society planting out flowers on a wet December day in 1984 in a scheme to improve the railway station approach. On the left, busy traffic on the A27 passes under the more functional railway bridge which replaced the former arched stone structure.

embankment south of West Street, then across the Gosport Road and the lower parts of Portland and Quay Streets and over the upper reaches of the creek by way of an impressive series of many-arched viaducts. The line progressed towards Portsmouth over Bridgefoot and under Downend Lane before reaching the brick-and-flint Portchester station, built in the style of a castle to reflect the village's connection with its Roman fortress.

Thus, within a decade, Portsmouth, Southampton and even London had come within relatively easy reach of Fareham folk. Rail travel was not cheap at first – unless one was prepared to ride in the open trucks of third class – but the Railways Act of 1844 reduced the costs by compelling the companies to run at least one train each weekday at a fare of only 1d. per mile. The third-class accommodation on the LSWR was quickly improved and by 1850 was described as the finest in England. In 1851, when excursions were organised to the Great Exhibition, many Fareham residents took a train to London for the first time in their lives to gaze in awe at the sights not only of the exhibition, but also of the capital itself.

More railway development followed. In 1889 a new direct line to Southampton via Swanwick and Bursledon was constructed, joining the Fareham line a little north of the station. Then, in 1903, the Meon Valley line, via Wickham and Droxford to Alton and London, was built, linking up to Fareham via Knowle Junction. This new line was welcomed not only by passengers from the distant villages but particularly by local farmers, as is illustrated by the strong support for the new railway from the Fareham and Hampshire Farmers Club. At this time there were still extensive farms and market gardens north of Fareham, and the agriculturalists were delighted to despatch their produce in the convenient trains. Milk was sent to all parts, cattle and other livestock were brought to the weekly markets in Fareham and Alton whilst, during the season, vast quantities of strawberries were loaded at Mislingford and Wickham.

The new routes into Fareham necessitated changes in the station layout. Island platforms had been added in 1889, and access to the new platforms was made easier when the road bridge carrying the lines to Gosport and Portsmouth was altered and strengthened by the addition of an extra arch; between the two arches was a flight of steps which led direct to a gateway on the platform where tickets could be issued and checked. There were large goods sheds on the eastern side of the station, while opposite the up platform were livestock sheds and pens.

Intriguingly, Fareham might have had yet another railway route. During the 1870s a company was formed with the intention of constructing a branch line from Fareham to Hill Head, where it was proposed that a harbour and pier should be built for boat services to Cowes. This scheme, known as the Cowes, Hill Head & London Railway, was promoted by three local businessmen, Alexander More, James Withers and William Mansell, while the chief engineer was Richard Saunders. The idea was to link the Isle of Wight to London directly, via Fareham. The company planned that the new link should leave the existing Fareham to Gosport line just south of the Redlands Lane railway arch, thence swinging southwestward through land occupied in 2006 by houses in St Michael's Grove, Fairfield Avenue and Longfield Avenue. Next, the proposed new railway would cross Mays Lane and Titchfield Road, near the Holy Rood Church at Crofton, before running parallel with Old Street and Titchfield Haven to the new pier. In 1874 the plans were agreed in Parliament and became the Fareham Railway Act. Despite the official sanction, however, the track was never laid. Difficulties regarding the provision of either a bridge or a level crossing over Titchfield Road, together with generally mounting costs and the fact that there were already other routes in place for islanders to get to London, meant that ultimately

Knowle asylum was provided with a halt on the Fareham to Eastleigh railway line in May 1907. This is the signal box at Knowle, situated at the junction with the Meon Valley line which led off to Wickham, Droxford and beyond. The signal box was closed in 1973.

A painting by Susan Musselwhite showing a tram on its way to the West End terminus near the railway station, having just passed Pyle's Temperance Hotel and the Royal Oak inn. Along this section of West Street, the tramlines were single.

the company was dissolved and the thoroughly planned and surveyed railway line was never built.

Although no one would have believed it at the time, the early years of the twentieth century marked the zenith of Fareham's importance as a railway centre. A fine station, busy with passengers and goods, stood unchallenged as a modern transportation centre at the entrance to a growing and prosperous town. The first hint of competition for the railway's monopoly, however, appeared in 1905, when the Provincial tram company abandoned its horse-drawn vehicles, which operated in Gosport, and replaced them with an electric tramway extending all the way to Fareham. The Provincial company built a power station at Hoeford and soon the overhead lines carrying the current, together with the rails along which the trams were to run, were constructed. Starting from Gosport Hard, the tramway was built alongside what is now the A32, entering Fareham underneath the railway viaduct, up Portland Street and along West Street to a terminus originally some 200 yards from the railway station. The first electric tram ran between Fareham and Gosport in December 1905, the inaugural public service commencing on 24 January 1906 with driver Bob Heath and conductor Jim May in charge of the first tram between the two towns. Soon the terminus was moved westwards to the West Street Inn, situated even nearer to the station. The new tram services ran from here to Gosport every 15 minutes at a cost of 4d. As the trams not only linked the two towns' railway stations but also passed through or quite near to the main shopping centres, they quickly became very popular. The fleet of 22 emerald green and cream vehicles were beautifully maintained and provided a striking sight in the busy town centres. The long-established railway route between Fareham and Gosport suffered a decline in use, particularly as both the railway stations in both towns were somewhat out on a limb, some distance away from the centres of the communities they served.

One group for whom the railway line to Gosport was quite convenient, however, were the pupils of that town's grammar school in Clarence Road, not far from the Spring Garden Lane terminus. Many schoolchildren travelled in by rail from Botley or the Meon Valley station, as well as from Fareham. In 1916, a girl writing in the school magazine presented this amusing account of Fareham station at that time:

It is quite a usual thing in the morning to find six green-capped girls in a group behind the bookstall, their satchels piled on the seat behind them. If it is cold, a move is made to the other end of the platform, where three or four pillars and a long seat serve admirably for a game of tag (the waiting rooms are being swept out and we are not allowed inside). By the time the down train runs in we are quite warm and ready to 'do our bit'. This 'bit' is looked upon in various degrees of gratitude by the railway officials. Porters are so few in number that it takes quite a long time to move the luggage. We have never been told we are in the way, but much depends on the nature of the guard or whether the porters are hurried. Milk churns we are naturally not allowed to touch. Only once did we attempt to move a barrel, the contents of which were at first a mystery. Curiosity overcame us, so we made a tiny hole in the wet cloth cover, thus disclosing some small mackerel. It was with abated zeal we rolled that tub, and, alas, the hole got larger and at each twist a slippery fish slid to the platform.

Soon the railways were to be menaced by another new form of transport, the private motor vehicle. Its development was slow at first, the cost of early motoring limiting its use to the well-off. One of the first cars ever seen in the streets of Fareham was an 1895 Lutzmann, owned by Mr J. Kooson of Southsea.

RAILWAY DELIGHTS AND ROAD DISASTERS

West Street, c.1900, with the old Market Hall next to the fire station on the left. The horses, carts and carriages in the wide street almost give the impression of a small town in the American Wild West!

His wife wrote in her diary of the adventures they had with their new-fangled horseless carriage:

Dec. 9 1895. Drove to Lee at 10. Motor sparked at once and went well. After lunch, started for home, came round by Fareham, had lovely drive; police spotted us; awful crowd followed us at Cosham; had to beat them off with umbrella.
Dec. 10. Policeman called at 1.30, took our names re. driving through Fareham without red flag ahead.
Dec. 16. Took train to Fareham, met Hobbs (solicitor) and proceeded to Court House. Filthy place. Hobbs spoke up well for motors. Silly old magistrate fined us one shilling and costs, 15s.7d.

An inauspicious debut indeed for the new mode of transport, but soon a few more wealthy individuals began to acquire these machines. Some believed the noisy and unreliable vehicles would be but a passing craze, but others were more far-seeing. In 1905 the Fareham and Hampshire Farmers Club, perhaps mindful of the safety of their own animals on the roads, put forward a resolution that the speed of cars should not exceed 12m.p.h., reducing to 8m.p.h. in towns and villages. They also urged the need for proper registration of cars by way of the addition of distinctive numbers front and rear.

Many enterprising Fareham businessmen foresaw the coming age of the motor vehicle. Such bicycle shops as E. & C. Hunt's, Grafham & Sons and Huxford's, began to offer 'Pratt's Motor Spirit' and other early forms of petrol, as well as other car

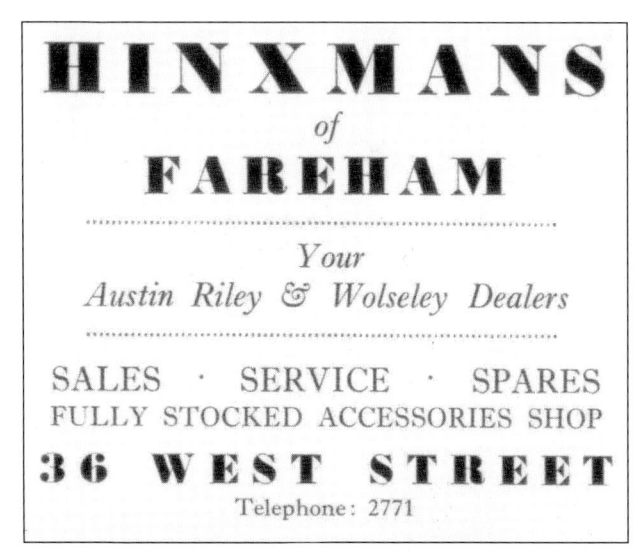

HINXMANS
of
FAREHAM

Your
Austin Riley & Wolseley Dealers

SALES · SERVICE · SPARES
FULLY STOCKED ACCESSORIES SHOP

36 WEST STREET
Telephone: 2771

An advertisement from the mid-1950s for E.J. Hinxman's garage, which was built on the site of the former Cole's coachbuilding works. Hinxman's served Fareham motorists for several decades. At the time of writing, the Ethel Austin clothes shop stands on this site.

accessories and repair facilities. The Red Lion Hotel started selling petrol and, in addition, provided garage accommodation. Hunt's large establishment at the bottom of High Street, next door to W.G. Abraham the upholsterer and furniture dealer, built and sold their very own 'Swallow' bicycles, besides providing a range of services for motorists. This shop was taken over by Charlie May who, just after the First World War, became one of the area's first

Local haulier Fred Dyke with his horse, Teddy, and wagon outside his house, 'Roughay', in Osborn Road in the 1930s.

Dyke's haulage firm promised to go 'Anywhere with Anything'. Here are members of his workforce with three steam-powered vehicles near the railway arches, where the firm stored its equipment. Fred Dyke also owned a garage and repair shop at Lower Quay.

❖ RAILWAY DELIGHTS AND ROAD DISASTERS ❖

Herbert Rogers (left), c.1910, and Mr Miles on one of their milk rounds in the town. The milk was delivered from the large churn into the householders' own jugs. Miles's Dairy operated from Abshot Road at this time. Eventually, the well-known and well-loved local farmer Tom Parker bought up most of the smaller milk rounds and established the famous dairy business so familiar in Fareham for several decades.

A young lad glances at the camera as Charlie Smith's bus passes in front of Fontley brickworks, c.1927. Charlie Smith and his brother Albert operated the Fareham, Fontley and Knowle bus service from 1926. Provincial bought the Smith Brothers' company in the 1950s.

motorcycle dealers. By the early 1920s motorists' needs in Fareham were served by more specialist garages, such as those of Richard Goodall and E.J. Hinxman, situated at opposite ends of West Street. Goodall was an agent for Ford cars and also offered vehicles for hire; Hinxman's offered complete motor overhauls, with 'painting and upholstering executed by competent workmen on the premises.' The latter garage occupied the same site which had once produced an earlier form of transport, namely Cole's the coach-builder. Other Fareham firms were alert to the new technology. Fred Dyke's haulage business adopted both steam- and petrol-driven lorries to improve his services; in the 1920s the vehicles were stored under the arches of the railway viaduct. Another Fareham haulier, Harry Luckett, set up in business in 1926, later starting bus and coach services which still flourish in 2006, proudly bearing the family name.

During the 1920s Fareham's wide main roads began to assume a very different character as more cars and lorries joined the horse-drawn vehicles and electric trams. As the development of motor vehicles carried on apace and engines became more reliable, the electric trams themselves came under threat from enterprising local firms who began to run bus services. Names such as Mallard, Tutt, the Smith Brothers, Fuger, Moore and the Enterprise Co.

A fascinating photograph of activity at the bus station in 1945, when servicemen mingled with smartly-dressed shoppers. A Provincial double-decker is travelling up Portland Street, while the former Methodist Church on the far right has scaffolding around it.

The bus station viewed from Portland Street in the late 1940s. Behind the two Hants & Dorset buses stands the former Methodist Church, while the large building to the right is the Savoy Cinema, which was to be replaced in the 1950s by the new Woolworth's.

An advertisement from 1955 for Provincial bus services. The vehicle depicted is a Bedford-Duple coach, bought in 1954, which remained in service in the area until 1968.

appeared on the sides of new buses to rival the trams. The new firms ran services to and from the more outlying districts, where the tramlines did not reach; for example, Charlie Smith provided buses for Fontley and Knowle via Fareham. Eventually, larger companies – Hants & Dorset, Southdown and Provincial themselves – bought out most of the smaller operators, although Smith Brothers' services continued until the 1950s. Provincial abandoned their electric trams on the last day of 1929, beginning the new decade with a fleet of petrol-driven buses which included some six-wheeled Chevrolets. The company was compelled to pay the costs of removing the tramlines and resurfacing the roads, a massive £40,000. Many local people mourned the loss of their tramways, which had given Fareham's town centre a character all its own, and the early bus trips to Gosport were often rough rides due to the wretched condition of the roads between the towns. However, the popular green Provincial buses were here to stay for another six decades, until the company was bought by FirstBus in 1995. At the time of writing the operation of local buses is undertaken by First Hampshire & Dorset Ltd, a subsidiary of FirstBus.

✣ RAILWAY DELIGHTS AND ROAD DISASTERS ✣

James, Charles and Sue Musselwhite at the bus station in March 1986 with three Provincial buses in the background.

Before the pedestrian precinct was extended, traffic could still use Portland Street to leave the town centre. There was a bus-stop outside the Savoy Buildings, towards which this Provincial bus is travelling along West Street in the 1980s.

The modern bus station, pictured from Hartlands Road in 2005, dwarfed by the backs of Fareham's new shops.

Taken from Radford's the ironmonger's at the corner of Quay Street, this 1948 view shows shoppers and traffic on a Saturday morning. Note the parking area in the middle of West Street, a facility that existed for many years.

Another Saturday morning, taken almost a decade later than the view above right from the same place. The most obvious change from the 1948 view is the increase in traffic along the north side of West Street, which continued to remain a problem until the relief roads to the south were constructed.

77

The Quay roundabout in August 1987. In the background, the Monday market is in full swing.

The Quay roundabout, photographed from the overbridge in a position similar to that of the picture on the left, but 18 years later, in 2005. The new Market Quay shops, cafés and cinema now provide a backdrop to the busy roundabout.

This view of the Quay roundabout from July 2005 illustrates the great effort that the Borough Council has made to improve this mundane facility with the planting and tending of attractive flower beds and shrubs – although the traffic around it is so frantic it is unlikely that many motorists have the time to enjoy these features.

However, thanks to the sterling efforts of a number of local enthusiasts, the name of Provincial lives on in the form of the Provincial Society. Formed in July 2004 under the chairmanship of John Sherwin, the society has actively promoted interest in the history of local buses by way of attendance at rallies, special trips on preserved green Provincial buses and such events as the special exhibition held at Westbury Manor Museum in September 2004.

Fareham's first bus station was built in 1931. In order to make room for it, several cottages, including the one in which the novelist Thackeray had spent some of his childhood, were demolished. At that time the large Methodist Church stood next door to the new bus station, but in 1954 this was demolished so that the bus station could be enlarged and an entrance from Hartlands Road provided. For many years the bus station, shared by Hants & Dorset, Southdown and Provincial, dominated this area of the south side of West Street. By the last decade of the century there was plenty of space for the buses, but the vast and ever-increasing number of cars had outstripped the parking places in the town. Consequently, a new bus station was built with both entrance and exit links to Hartlands Road, while its former site was developed into a large car park. This, too, vanished beneath the buildings which front Fareham's Market Quay development.

Today's transport problems in and around Fareham are, of course, entirely due to the huge numbers of cars, lorries and vans which bring the inadequate roads to a standstill many times in a day. Most people, it seems, while bemoaning both the dangers on our roads and the dreary gridlocks that occur so frequently, still would not dream of being without the convenience that a car affords. While a really efficient public transport system would certainly help matters, apathy, economics and organised opposition from vested interests have brought about a decline in this area, particularly in the railway sector. For example, the useful railway link to Gosport was closed as long ago as 1953, just at a time when major new housing developments were being built between the two towns and the ownership of a car was within the reach of many more families. The Meon Valley line was closed in February 1955, also forcing travellers and goods onto the roads. Thankfully, Fareham still has its railway station – although the road lobby would have had it closed years ago – and its services have improved, in large part thanks to the electrification of the lines to Southampton and Eastleigh. It is a pity that planners could not have come up with some form of transport interchange between rail and bus at the station – it is a long walk between the two.

The bold initiative of the Light Rail Transit scheme, carefully planned and developed since the late-twentieth century, is an attempt to alleviate some of the awful congestion along the roads between Fareham and Gosport by running trams along part of the former trackbed of the railway between the towns and extending beneath the harbour to

RAILWAY DELIGHTS AND ROAD DISASTERS

Looking east across the Quay roundabout from the over-bridge, c. 1980, before the flyover was built. The skyline is dominated by the foundry chimneys and the gasometer.

Taken from the same location in 2005 as the picture on the left, the foundry and the gasometer are no more, and ugly road markings and the flyover catch the eye. It is interesting to note the phenomenal growth of the trees on the roundabout in the last quarter of a century.

The Gosport Road entrance to the Quay roundabout in 2005. The railway arches carried the lines which have taken people speedily to their destinations for over 150 years; the road flyover and the roundabout represent modern attempts to achieve at least something better than traffic gridlock.

Hartlands Road, looking towards West Street, in August 1987. Road alterations and the extended bus station have changed this scene – the houses on the right are gone, and traffic is busy here.

Portsmouth. At the time of writing, the scheme has been rejected again by the Labour government, despite the fact that even the reduced version of the plan would obviously have considerable value in reducing traffic on our roads. Will we ever see trams run again on the streets of Fareham, or even perhaps a guided busway, or are we headed for gridlock on our existing inadequate roads? While the government in power claims to pursue green transport policies yet lamentably fails to support such carefully planned schemes as the Light Rail Transit, it seems that it will be the latter grim fate that awaits us here.

Bath Lane recreation ground, opened under the auspices of the council in 1887, pictured here in 1974. The removal of the gasometer has since enhanced the outlook.

Fareham Town became the leading local football team, playing at various times in the Hampshire League, Southern League and Wessex League. In 1978 the club moved from Bath Lane to the new Cams Alders Sports Centre. This picture taken from the grandstand in 1987 shows play in progress between Fareham Town and Fisher Athletic in a Southern League match.

Many Fareham shops and firms had their own sports teams. Here the players of Pyle's bakery football team pose proudly for the camera in 1921. Players include: Edward Clark (top left) next to William Bundey, George Colebourne (top right), George Hobbs (bottom left) and Mr Coombes (seated centre).

✦ CHAPTER 10 ✦

Leisure and Pleasure

Leisure time is something we all take for granted today. It was not always so, especially for what used to be termed 'the working class'. Many of the opportunities to play rather than work for such people came about as a result of statutory reductions in working hours during the late Victorian period, together with a general increase in prosperity at this time. In the 1880s, for example, sport was being played on a more regular and organised basis, many teams developing from church, chapel and shop roots. Fareham Cricket Club was organised initially by the curate of the Parish Church, Revd F.J. Ashmall. Originally, the club played its matches on a small piece of ground behind Trinity Church, but by the early 1900s, along with many other sports teams, it had moved its home to the recreation ground at Bath Lane. By the creek, this very pleasant venue for sports of all kinds was opened in 1887 and extended in 1903 by the council. The Fareham Hockey Club played there too, as did such soccer teams as Fareham Wednesday – so named because that day of the week was a half-day off for many shops – and Pyle's FC, whose team consisted of workers from the bakery of that name. Over the years, Fareham Town FC became established as the borough's premier team. Having played for many years at Bath Lane, the town team moved to the new Cams Alders ground in 1978. Great excitement prevailed in November 1988 when Fareham entertained Barclays League side Torquay United in a replay of the first round proper of the FA Cup, going down 2–3 before a huge all-ticket crowd and the television cameras.

No doubt local people enjoyed themselves just as much, when they could, in more distant times,

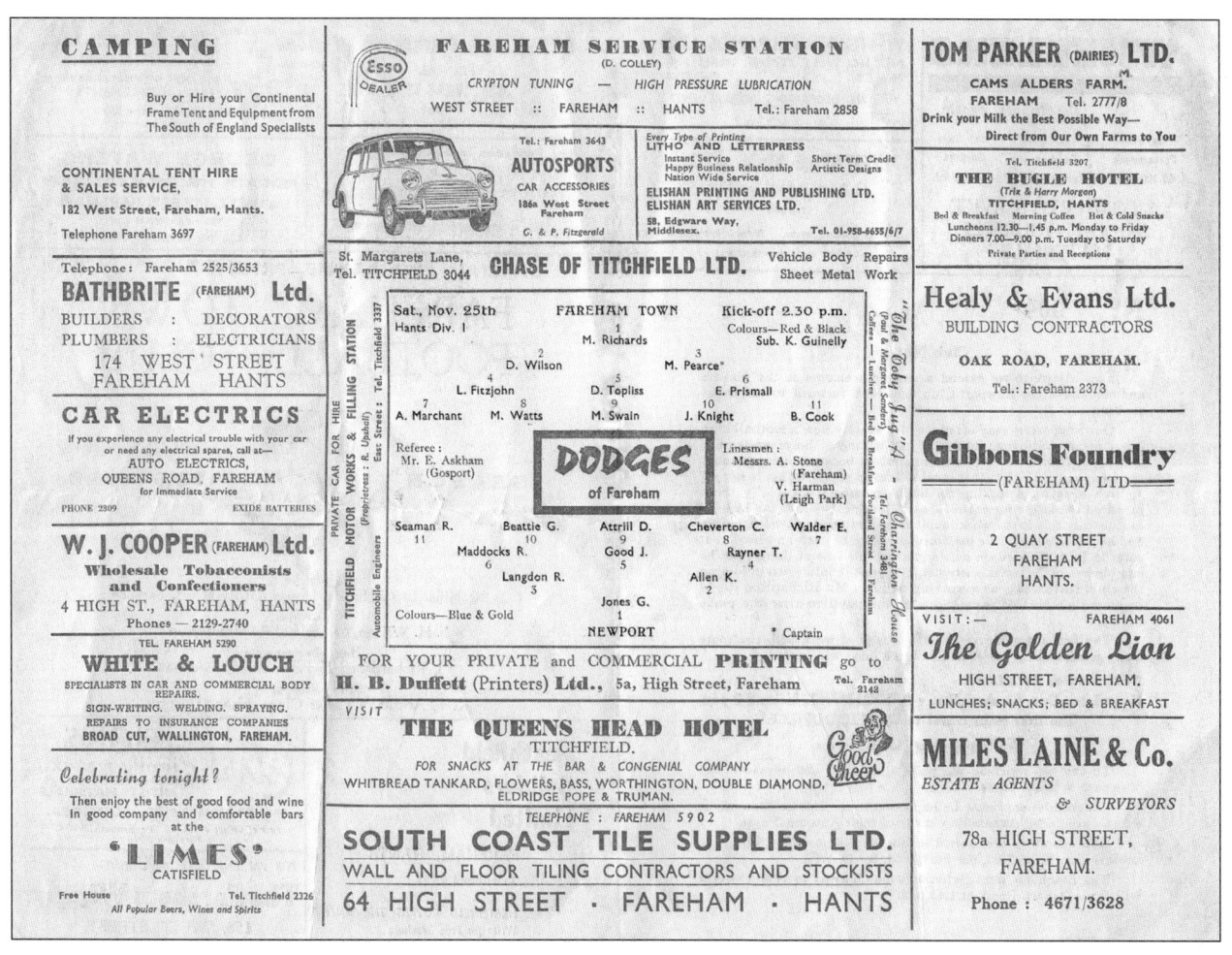

The centre spread of Fareham Town FC's programme for 25 November 1967 of a Hampshire League fixture against Newport, Isle of Wight. Most of the businesses advertising their wares here are now but a memory, although a few still serve the local public.

The eighteenth-century Red Lion Hotel on a cold December day in 2005. This fine hostelry once contained a ballroom with a musician's gallery and has always been a popular venue for public and private functions.

A once popular venue for balls, dances, meetings and entertainments, the Portland Hall, now solicitors' offices, is seen here in October 2005.

though opportunities to let off steam were few and far between. The only regular holidays in medieval times were the Church days of Easter, Christmas and Whitsun. Fareham folk probably had most fun at the annual two-day fair in June, with its crockery and china stalls, rides, peepshows and hawkers selling ribbons, toys, hats and sweets. Quite often the fair days culminated in a procession through the streets down to the waterside, where robust water sports took place to conclude the festivities. The presence of the sea has, of course, always ensured some leisure activity on the water. It is known that as long ago as 1850, a Fareham Rowing Club was flourishing. Later this became the Fareham Sailing Club, with J.T. See acting as its first Commodore; in 1931 the name was changed to Fareham Sailing & Motor Boat Club, with Captain MacDonald of Belvoir House in charge. During the early 1980s the club revived the old-style regattas, to great public acclaim.

Many people preferred quieter leisure pursuits. An early attempt to provide a forum for intellectual discussion was the establishment in 1834, by a group of worthies led by the then vicar of Holy Trinity church, Revd Henry Thompson, of the Society for Literary and Philosophical Objects. The society raised considerable funds to build a permanent venue for the presentation of lectures and talks. The resulting building was the magnificent Portland Hall, opened by the Chancellor, Lord Brougham, in 1835. The society, it seems, did not last long, and by the 1850s the great white stone building, with its Ionic columns, was being used as a Town Hall, with some of its rooms sub-let for other events. The top floor, seating 400, has been used by Fareham's choral and dramatic societies, while other entertainments, including dances, have often been held there. In the early years of the last century, solicitors Goble & Warner, the forerunners of the present incumbents, had their offices in Portland Hall, which also housed the Fareham Working Men's Club and the local council meetings.

The Red Lion Hotel, first recorded in 1784 as an excise office and as offering post-chaises for hire under the proprietorship of Thomas Hewlett, was also a venue for social events for the better-off citizens of Fareham. Concerts and assemblies, as well as meetings, were frequently held there in the nineteenth century. One group which held its discussions there was the splendidly named South East Hants Association for the Encouragement of Industrious and Meritorious Agricultural Labourers, a society whose officers included such local worthies as H.P. Delme, James Thresher and Charles Osborn. A fascinating history of this old inn is to be found in Malcolm Low's excellent book, *The Red Lion Hotel, Fareham: An Eighteenth Century Coaching Inn*.

A general spirit of self-help and self-improvement in the second half of the nineteenth century led to the development of clubs and societies where like-minded people could come together for mutual support and friendship in a social situation. Such new groups as the Oddfellows' Lodge and the Ancient Order of Foresters met on a regular basis, the former usually at the Royal Oak, the latter in their imposing Foresters' Hall of 1881. The Fareham and County Club was established at No. 18 West Street and, during the last century, the Freemasons had their hall in Queens Road. Besides these places, such venues as the church halls, the Assembly Hall and the Connaught Hall continued to be used for social occasions of all types.

Music-making was mostly the preserve of church and chapel in earlier times; for example, the choral group of St Peter and St Paul's held regular meetings at the Market Hall in the nineteenth century. In 1898, however, a group of local music-lovers led by Eugene

❖ LEISURE AND PLEASURE ❖

The ancient meadow and woodland area known as 'The Gillies' is a surprisingly large open space stretching from West Street to Redlands Lane. Once known as the Gully Field, the little river which runs through it was sometimes called the Gully Brook. The Fareham Society has done much valuable work in promoting conservation and interest in the area.

In May 2005 Penny Garrett contemplates the tranquil waters from the bridge along the walkway in The Gillies. The little railway arch which carries the main Fareham to Portsmouth line can be glimpsed in the distance.

Young local volunteers engaged in clean-up operations in The Gillies.

Spinney, organist at St Peter and St Paul's, formed the Fareham Philharmonic Society with the declared aim of developing 'public knowledge of the appreciation of classical music by public performance.' How delighted Eugene Spinney and the other founder members would have been to see the continuing success of the society today. The new society's first concert was performed in the Church of St Peter and St Paul on 25 April 1899. The programme presented was ambitious and included Mendelssohn's *Hymn of Praise*, Dvorak's *Te Deum* and Parry's *Blest Pair of Sirens*, the latter two choral works being quite new at the time. The concert was attended by the staggering number of 800 enthusiastic music lovers. One of the singers at this opening concert, Harry Privett, remained a member of the society for an incredible 75 years. Interestingly, in 1998, the society celebrated its centenary by repeating the works performed at the inaugural concert at the same church, together with an extra piece, the *Magnificat*, written by local composer Stanley Browning. A former deputy conductor and pianist with the Fareham Philharmonic for many years, Mr Browning had also served both St Peter and St Paul's and Holy Trinity Churches as a chorister and organist. The society has enjoyed a long and successful life and continues to delight audiences with several public performances each year.

Another notable local entertainment organisation is the Fareham Musical Society, founded by Betty Richards in 1983. Originally under the musical direction of Maureen Tapping, this popular group has produced many light operas and stage musicals over the last 20 years, mostly at the Ferneham Hall. This venue has also been the adopted home since 1989 of Gosport Amateur Operatic Society. These music groups, together with the performers in the highly regarded annual Fareham Music Festival, have helped provide a high standard of music in the town for many years.

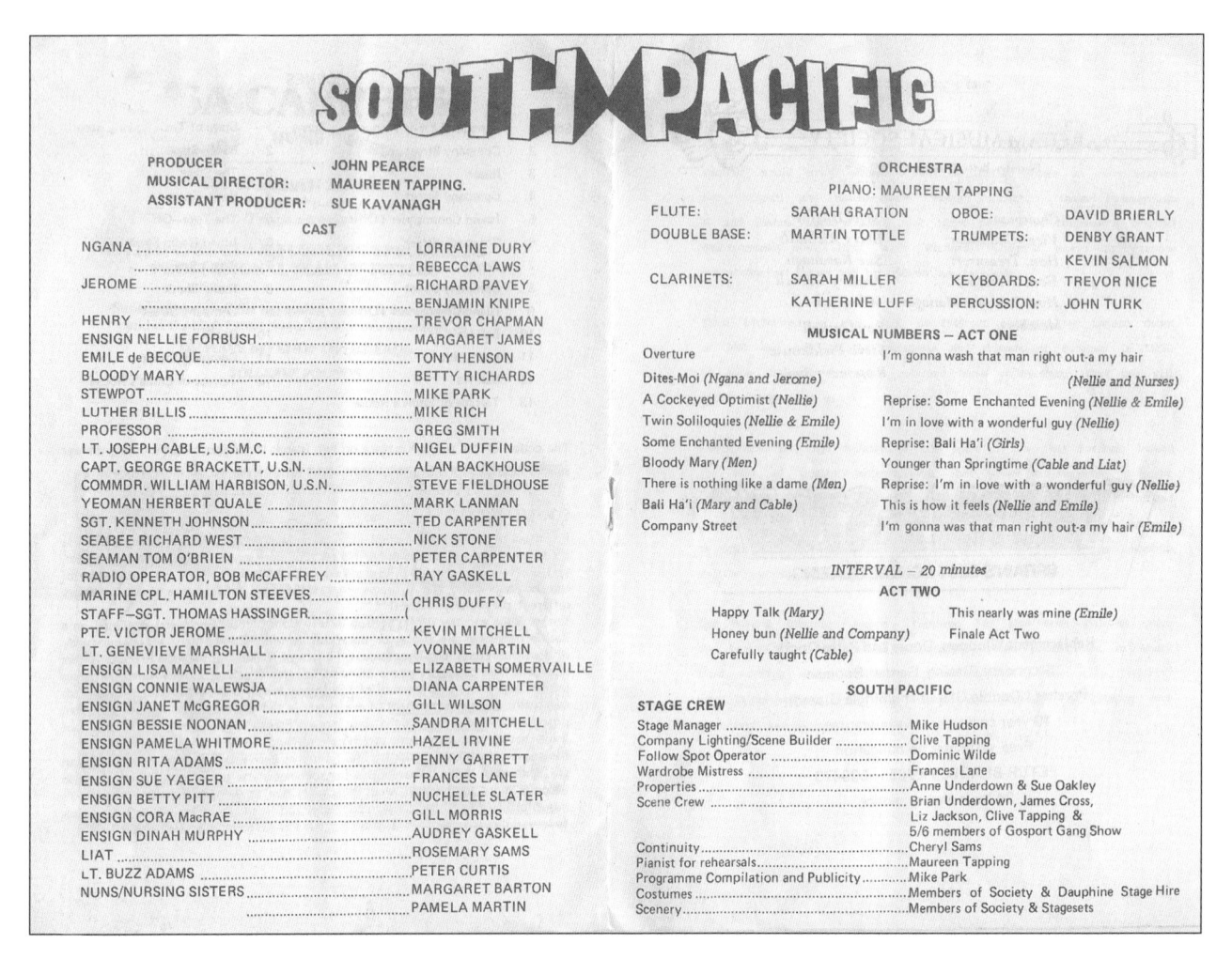

SOUTH PACIFIC

PRODUCER JOHN PEARCE
MUSICAL DIRECTOR: MAUREEN TAPPING.
ASSISTANT PRODUCER: SUE KAVANAGH

CAST

NGANA	LORRAINE DURY
	REBECCA LAWS
JEROME	RICHARD PAVEY
	BENJAMIN KNIPE
HENRY	TREVOR CHAPMAN
ENSIGN NELLIE FORBUSH	MARGARET JAMES
EMILE de BECQUE	TONY HENSON
BLOODY MARY	BETTY RICHARDS
STEWPOT	MIKE PARK
LUTHER BILLIS	MIKE RICH
PROFESSOR	GREG SMITH
LT. JOSEPH CABLE, U.S.M.C.	NIGEL DUFFIN
CAPT. GEORGE BRACKETT, U.S.N.	ALAN BACKHOUSE
COMMDR. WILLIAM HARBISON, U.S.N.	STEVE FIELDHOUSE
YEOMAN HERBERT QUALE	MARK LANMAN
SGT. KENNETH JOHNSON	TED CARPENTER
SEABEE RICHARD WEST	NICK STONE
SEAMAN TOM O'BRIEN	PETER CARPENTER
RADIO OPERATOR, BOB McCAFFREY	RAY GASKELL
MARINE CPL. HAMILTON STEEVES	(CHRIS DUFFY
STAFF–SGT. THOMAS HASSINGER	(
PTE. VICTOR JEROME	KEVIN MITCHELL
LT. GENEVIEVE MARSHALL	YVONNE MARTIN
ENSIGN LISA MANELLI	ELIZABETH SOMERVAILLE
ENSIGN CONNIE WALEWSJA	DIANA CARPENTER
ENSIGN JANET McGREGOR	GILL WILSON
ENSIGN BESSIE NOONAN	SANDRA MITCHELL
ENSIGN PAMELA WHITMORE	HAZEL IRVINE
ENSIGN RITA ADAMS	PENNY GARRETT
ENSIGN SUE YAEGER	FRANCES LANE
ENSIGN BETTY PITT	NUCHELLE SLATER
ENSIGN CORA MacRAE	GILL MORRIS
ENSIGN DINAH MURPHY	AUDREY GASKELL
LIAT	ROSEMARY SAMS
LT. BUZZ ADAMS	PETER CURTIS
NUNS/NURSING SISTERS	MARGARET BARTON
	PAMELA MARTIN

ORCHESTRA
PIANO: MAUREEN TAPPING

FLUTE:	SARAH GRATION	OBOE:	DAVID BRIERLY
DOUBLE BASE:	MARTIN TOTTLE	TRUMPETS:	DENBY GRANT
			KEVIN SALMON
CLARINETS:	SARAH MILLER	KEYBOARDS:	TREVOR NICE
	KATHERINE LUFF	PERCUSSION:	JOHN TURK

MUSICAL NUMBERS – ACT ONE

Overture
Dites-Moi *(Ngana and Jerome)*
A Cockeyed Optimist *(Nellie)*
Twin Soliloquies *(Nellie & Emile)*
Some Enchanted Evening *(Emile)*
Bloody Mary *(Men)*
There is nothing like a dame *(Men)*
Bali Ha'i *(Mary and Cable)*
Company Street

I'm gonna wash that man right out-a my hair
(Nellie and Nurses)
Reprise: Some Enchanted Evening *(Nellie & Emile)*
I'm in love with a wonderful guy *(Nellie)*
Reprise: Bali Ha'i *(Girls)*
Younger than Springtime *(Cable and Liat)*
Reprise: I'm in love with a wonderful guy *(Nellie)*
This is how it feels *(Nellie and Emile)*
I'm gonna was that man right out-a my hair *(Emile)*

INTERVAL – 20 minutes

ACT TWO

Happy Talk *(Mary)*   This nearly was mine *(Emile)*
Honey bun *(Nellie and Company)*   Finale Act Two
Carefully taught *(Cable)*

SOUTH PACIFIC
STAGE CREW

Stage Manager	Mike Hudson
Company Lighting/Scene Builder	Clive Tapping
Follow Spot Operator	Dominic Wilde
Wardrobe Mistress	Frances Lane
Properties	Anne Underdown & Sue Oakley
Scene Crew	Brian Underdown, James Cross, Liz Jackson, Clive Tapping & 5/6 members of Gosport Gang Show
Continuity	Cheryl Sams
Pianist for rehearsals	Maureen Tapping
Programme Compilation and Publicity	Mike Park
Costumes	Members of Society & Dauphine Stage Hire
Scenery	Members of Society & Stagesets

The cast, orchestra and stage crew of the September 1986 Fareham Music Society production of the musical South Pacific *at the Ferneham Hall.*

The Ferneham Hall itself was built between 1979 and 1982. Conceived as a multi-purpose hall, this function is still maintained today with such events as craft and collectors' fairs, model railway exhibitions and amateur musical and theatrical productions, as well as professional shows and entertainments and performances by well-known celebrities. The project, originally estimated to cost £1 million, was criticised by some local Labour councillors, who claimed that Fareham needed more community and sports halls instead of what they claimed was a prestige project. As the foundations were laid – handicapped by the builders' discovery that the soil was full of tree stumps, rusty metal and any amount of old rubbish – suggestions for a name for the new facility were passed around. Though the project had been commonly referred to as the 'Civic Hall', some interesting names

The Ferneham Hall, February 2005. As well as professional productions, the hall is also the venue for local amateur groups, as its founders always planned. The large banner advertises a forthcoming production by the Stage One Youth Theatre Company; the smaller invites shoppers to call in for tea or coffee.

The entrance to the Ferneham Hall, with the coffee lounge on the left, January 2005.

✦ LEISURE AND PLEASURE ✦

Members of the chorus of the Gosport Amateur Operatic Society perform a dress rehearsal at Ferneham Hall of their production of Kiss Me Kate, *November 1995. Left to right: Debbie Hughes, Peter Vale, Vicky Bradford, Tim Cole, Hilary Westbrook, Peter Coombes, Penny Garrett, Brian Musselwhite, Charlotte Dennison, Tony Scripps and Jim Mackman.*

(JOHN WESTBROOK)

The dress rehearsal of Gosport Amateur Operatic Society's production at Ferneham Hall of The Gondoliers *in May 1997. Left to right: Bill Delicate (Luiz), Anne Parker (Duchess of Plaza-Toro), Penny Garrett (Casilda) and Brian Musselwhite (Duke of Plaza-Toro).*

(JOHN WESTBROOK)

The Ashcroft Arts Centre, seen from the parish churchyard in December 2005. This venue for music, film, dance and other arts, formerly known as the Fareham and Gosport Drama Centre, was Fareham County Primary School for most of the twentieth century.

Part of the foyer of the 1930s Embassy Cinema in 1983. The posters feature a Wings appeal on behalf of the Royal Air Force Association and a competition to win a Honda scooter as part of a promotion for the film Flashdance.

Fareham's first cinema for over 20 years, the five-screen Apollo, in February 2005. The Apollo showed its first films in the summer of that year. To the left is another of Fareham's leisure attractions, the Chicago Rock Cafe.

were put forward: Osborn Hall, Citizens' Hall, Chequers, Mountbatten Hall, The Pleasure Centre and Queen Mother Hall were all considered. The names Gardner Hall and Rosemary Pockley Hall were also put forward, in honour of Peggy Gardner, leader of Fareham Borough Council, and the mayor, Rosemary Pockley. Though both had been enthusiastic supporters of the new hall, they declined the honour. Finally, the council decided to adopt the name Ferneham Hall, the thought being that the old name for the town would conjure a less mundane image than simply Fareham Hall.

The new hall opened in February 1982 with a gala weekend which included appearances on stage by Cilla Black and Don Maclean. Everyone wanted to visit Ferneham Hall in the first couple of months. A cabaret and dance, a boxing-club dinner, appearances by the Southampton All-Stars Band, the Royal Marine Band and the Andrews Sisters, together with a performance of *The Messiah* by the Fareham Philharmonic Society, were all well attended. Large crowds watched the official opening ceremony, performed in April by the Duchess of Kent. After this honeymoon period, however, local interest waned. By July, reports in the local press suggested that the new hall was not doing well. A trade fair was organised in September to boost local interest and an intensive leaflet campaign was organised in an attempt to stimulate patronage. The crisis passed and improvements began in the hall's fortunes when locals were asked to make suggestions for what they would like to see. Such big names as Harry Secombe, Val Doonican, Maddy Prior and Tom O'Connor drew the audiences, while Sotheby's organised an 'Antiques Roadshow'-style auction day. After the closure of Fareham's last cinema, the Embassy, in 1983, Ferneham Hall began to show films for the first time.

Now over 20 years old, Ferneham Hall has become a familiar landmark. Despite many ups and downs in its career, it continues to provide the area with entertainments and functions in a comfortable setting. Another cultural venue is the nearby Ashcroft Arts Centre, housed in the former Fareham County Primary School, which has a theatre, dance and rehearsal rooms and gallery space. This venue has provided Fareham with drama, music, cabaret, dance and films since 1979, when it began life as the Fareham and Gosport Drama Centre.

Although, as we have seen, film fans were able to watch movies at both Ferneham Hall and the Ashcroft from time to time, Fareham was without a purpose-built cinema between 1983, when the Embassy was closed and demolished, and 2005, when the five-screen Apollo opened in Market Quay. The first cinema in the town, known as the Electrical Theatre, was opened in 1910 on the site of an old chapel in West Street. Its outward appearance changed greatly over the years, and it was also a home for other entertainments, but in 1923 it was

✤ LEISURE AND PLEASURE ✤

In the early 1950s Fareham still had two cinemas: the Savoy (on the right), and the Embassy (the tall building behind the flagpole of the Savoy Buildings centre right). The bus station is to the left of the pedestrian crossing. Woolworth's, later W.H. Smith, is in the centre of the Savoy Buildings.

reborn as the Alexandra and, from that time onward, continued as a movie theatre. In 1938 it was replaced by the Embassy cinema, a striking building typical of the cinema architecture of that time, with a tall tower containing three porthole windows on each side of a set of white pillars. By this time, Fareham had another modern cinema, the Savoy, a notable endpiece to the group of white buildings of that name that opened in 1933. Both the Embassy and the Savoy, once so popular with local people, followed the same path into decline once the new medium of television became universal. The Savoy closed first and was demolished to make way for the large new Woolworth's store built to replace the original one in the centre of Savoy Buildings. When the Embassy was demolished in 1983, the site was used for that fast-growing fast-food phenomenon, McDonald's.

In the early years of the twentieth century, Fareham's library was, most appropriately, housed in Thackeray House, the bay-windowed building where the great novelist had stayed as a boy. After this house was demolished, however, Fareham's readers had to make do with seeking edification on the shelves of the cramped building popularly known as The Flying Angel, which had acted as a mission hall for servicemen during the Second World War. However, one of the boons provided in the first phase of Fareham's redevelopment was the planning of a brand-new library. The three-storey building which emerged, at a cost of £300,000, was the second largest in Hampshire, with a book stock numbering

Fareham Library in 2005.

97,000. The first chief librarian was Keith Hayward, who had a staff of 14 full-time and seven part-time assistants. At the official opening, on 24 July 1973, Lord Porchester unveiled a plaque in the foyer and was presented with a book by the youngest member of staff, Carole Edwards. The library has continued to thrive and adapt to the changing needs of the community. In 2006, functioning as both loan and reference library, it is a facility of which Fareham may be justly proud.

That same accolade can also be accorded to Fareham's museum, which has served the town for more than 15 years. Westbury Manor, the home of

When the civic offices were built, the former council offices at Westbury Manor, seen here in 1979, were vacant for a time. Before the decision to turn the Manor into a museum was taken, various other ideas were discussed, including its possible conversion into a casino! The adjacent building at the corner of Hartlands Road was the council's banking hall.

Westbury Manor Museum, May 2005.

Westbury Manor in its early days as a museum. Note the new seat and flowerbed, and the former banking hall still in position.

The museum from its garden, May 2005.

Officials and guests in the garden of the museum in June 1994, when a delegation from Fareham's twin town in Germany, Pulheim, visited the museum to meet members of the council and the Fareham Society and to present a sundial in honour of the tenth anniversary of the twinning.

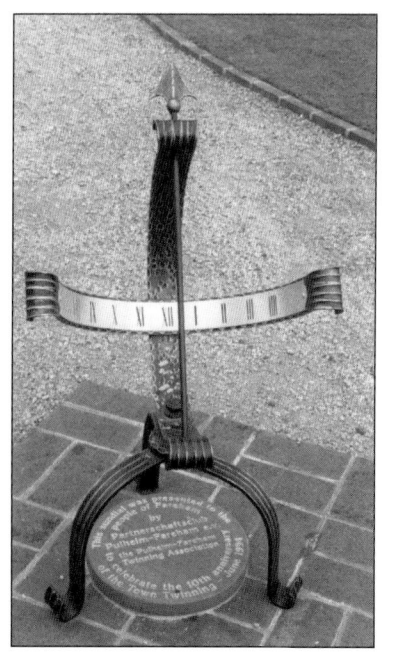

The Pulheim sundial, June 1994.

◈ LEISURE AND PLEASURE ◈

The former United Reformed Church in West Street undergoing renovation and extension work in May 2005 for its conversion into a bar/restaurant.

the museum, is one of Fareham's best-known and best-loved buildings. In the seventeenth century it was a farmhouse which, during the next two centuries, was considerably altered and extended. It became an elegant Georgian town house, and was the home over the years of no less than six admirals. In the twentieth century Westbury Manor had a new lease of life when it was used as the offices of Fareham Urban District Council between 1932 and 1976. After the local council had moved into the new civic offices, the old house stood forlorn and disused for many years until a kind bequest to the town proved, in a roundabout way, to be its saviour. Winifred Cocks left her home in Wickham Road to the borough for use as a museum under the terms of her will in 1979, but the council decided that this house was too far from the town centre to be convenient for this purpose. Instead the council sold the house and set up a trust from the proceeds with which, in partnership with Hampshire County Council, it was able to acquire Westbury Manor. The old building, renovated and restored, opened as the museum in 1990. It is a major focal point of local history, its fine collection enhanced by special exhibitions reflecting the social, natural and industrial history of Fareham. Westbury Manor also possesses a most pleasant coffee shop, which overlooks one of the town centre's quietest spots, the museum's Victorian-style garden. This garden, which replaced an untidy area of asphalt in 1993, provides an enclosed oasis of calm amidst the bustle of present-day Fareham.

Earlier we suggested that organised sporting activities were quick to develop in the days when increased leisure time became the norm. In the twenty-first century it seems that sports participation is stronger than ever. The Borough Council has to be commended for its initiatives with regard to sports facilities during the last 30 years; they have borne fruit. Park Lane has been the venue for many sporting activities, where both the bowling green, used by the Fareham Bowling Club, and the swimming pool, later enlarged into the Fareham Leisure Centre, with its health and fitness apparatus, squash, trampolining, badminton and other facilities, are appreciated by large numbers of people. Indeed, the choice of leisure activities in the area has never been more varied. The council operates a Fareham Leisure Card which, at the time of writing, offers discounts for a range of activities from 'Clever Cats', the children's music and mime group, to the popular 'Soccer City' at Broadcut.

Left: *Nurse Mary Cresswell astride her new bicycle, bought for her by grateful patients in 1932.*

Mr and Mrs W. Worlock with their son at Fareham Workhouse, c.1930. The Worlocks were in charge there from 1911 until 1931.

Members of a concert party at Fareham Workhouse, c.1920.

CHAPTER 11

Caring for the Sick

In earlier centuries the fear of disease loomed large in people's lives. The means of preventing or curing diseases were few and only on the rarest occasions could the ordinary labouring poor afford to pay for the services of a medical man. Indeed, the medical profession as we know it today barely existed before the middle of the nineteenth century. So how did the working people of a small town like Fareham cope with illness in the family?

Early town directories, particularly those of the eighteenth and nineteenth centuries, give us clues. Among the list of names that of the apothecary appears regularly. These persons were vital to ordinary families of limited means. Simple remedies based largely on herbs could be purchased from them, or small quantities of the basic ingredients could be kept in the family store cupboard and made up by the housewife when needed.

Childbirth in former times could be a very dangerous and life-threatening business for both mother and child. The woman in labour was usually attended by a female member of the family or a neighbour. Surprisingly, the Fareham town directories tell us that between 1784 and 1795, three male midwives were in practice in the town. These gentlemen were Mr George Fall, Mr John English and Mr Thomas Blatherwick, the latter also being entered as a surgeon. All were professional men and payment for their services would have been quite beyond the means of the poorest families.

Inspired, perhaps, by the example of Florence Nightingale, many women were coming forward in the latter part of the nineteenth century to train in nursing and midwifery. Nurse Mary Cresswell, one of Fareham's best loved midwives, was born in Soberton in 1865 and had to wait until 1905 to get her certification. Over a long career she was estimated to have delivered almost 3,000 babies to the grateful mothers of Fareham and district. In 1932 local supporters clubbed together to buy Nurse Cresswell a much-needed new bicycle. When she died in 1947 at the age of 81 her life and work were celebrated in the local press.

Fareham women would have to wait until well into the twentieth century before a modern and fully equipped maternity hospital became available. On 1 April 1950 the fine Georgian building of Blackbrook House opened as a maternity home with 20 beds in the charge of Matron Tapp, assisted by two or three sisters and staff midwives. Blackbrook also operated as a training school for midwives, the trainees living on the splendid premises.

In June 2000 a garden party was held at Blackbrook to celebrate 50 years of its existence. The first baby to be born there on, 9 April 1950, was Roger Anthony Pumphrey who, delighted to be asked to officially open the garden party, brought with him the silver cup presented to him as Blackbrook's first arrival. The maternity home was closed after this commemorative event but to general relief was re-opened the following year. At the time of writing it has been closed yet again but, like so many other communities, Fareham has continued to campaign for more hospital facilities of all kinds.

A century and a half ago dentistry was unknown to the general population, although not to the middle and upper classes. Queen Victoria often deplored the poor state of the teeth of her daughters' prospective husbands! For nearly everyone else, a tooth extraction was almost a bizarre form of entertainment, undertaken by itinerant tooth-pullers who were a ghoulish attraction at local fairs. Perhaps Fareham, like other communities at this time, welcomed these men. It would not be until the early years of the twentieth century that family dental practices were established in Fareham. It is worth recalling that it was not until 1889 that the first dental school in England was opened at Guy's Hospital in London.

The earliest recorded hospital in Fareham was at Lower Quay. Here a number of buildings were first used as a hospital for sick and wounded sailors when England was at war with the Dutch in the seventeenth century. By the eighteenth century the same buildings were used to house sick prisoners from the wars with France. At this period, Fareham was a significant maritime community and ships unloaded the men at the quay for basic care at this prison hospital. In recent years excavations have brought to light the skeletal remains of these unfortunate men.

The first institution to be built in Fareham, where albeit fairly primitive care was available, was the workhouse in Wickham Road, built in 1836 and run as a workhouse until taken over by the National Health Service in 1948, when it became a geriatric hospital (St Christopher's). In the immediate hand-over period the institution had about 35 bed patients and some 45 of the original workhouse inmates, who had no need of hospital care but had no other accommodation. Among these were approximately 20 women of various ages, some accompanied by their children. It was a requirement of the hand-over to the National Health Service that all able-bodied

Mr W. Worlock (seated, third row centre) *with the workhouse cricket team of 1930.*

The 1930 charity show on the lawns at Wickham Road workhouse. Both staff and inmates joined in these happy events.

inmates must leave as soon as possible and most had gone by 1950. Until that time they assisted in the day-to-day cleaning of the buildings and also looked after the garden. Five cells were allocated for tramps to sleep in overnight; before leaving the institution they were given certain tasks to perform to the satisfaction of the workhouse master. This man was in overall charge, aided by his wife as matron. She supervised 34 nurses and 14 ward maids, these dressed in wrap-around green overalls. Other non-medical staff were the two boiler men, a bricklayer, a boot repairer, porters and laundry staff. These last were paid a very respectable (at the time) wage of £5 a week. Their more unusual extra duties included looking after the piggeries, which had been a valuable source of meat for the old workhouse, roast pork being for many years the centrepiece of the institution's excellent Christmas dinners. These same porters collected the drugs from the Fareham pharmacy and were responsible for carrying buckets of coal for the wards' many fireplaces – pre-1950, only one ward was fitted with central heating. Porters had the potentially tricky task of bathing the sometimes reluctant 50 male inmates each week, a chore which was spread over three days!

Meals at St Christopher's 50 years ago were simple by today's standards but quite nourishing. Porridge, toast and marmalade for breakfast, boiled ham or a roast for dinner (thanks to the piggeries), bread and jam for tea and a supper of bread and cheese before lights out at 8p.m. A dumb waiter took the food to the upper floors. This internal system was discontinued in 1953, when the in-house catering was taken over by Portsmouth's Group Catering Manager. In the same year the old workhouse ethos finally came to an end when the first fully qualified National Health Service staff arrived. All the appurtenances that today's patients expect from a stay in hospital began to appear. Chiropody, hairdressing, confectionery and toilet items were introduced. Fareham's Red Cross and St John Ambulance crews provided other services, including trolleys of library books, and outings were organised for patients. The last surviving connection with the

British Red Cross Society and Order of St. John.

HOME SERVICE MOTOR AMBULANCE.

FAREHAM & RURAL DISTRICT.

Telephone: 8 a.m. to 8 p.m. week days, Fareham 194.
" 8 p.m. to 8 a.m. and Sundays, Fareham 6.

RULES.

1. The Ambulance is for the use of residents in the Fareham Union.

2. The Ambulance is garaged at Messrs. Bennett & Righton, West Street, Fareham, Tel. 194.

3. Application for the use of the Ambulance between 8 a.m. and 8 p.m. week days, is to be made to Messrs. Bennett & Righton, Tel. 194, and from 8 p.m. to 8 a.m. and on Sundays to the Police Station, Fareham, Tel. 6.

4. An emergency case will always take precedence to any other call.

5. The Charge will be 6d. for each mile travelled by the Ambulance with a minimum charge of 2/6. If the Ambulance is kept waiting for more than half-an-hour for, or after the removal of, the patient, a charge of 2/6 per hour will be made.

6. A statement of the charges for the use of the Ambulance will be rendered by the Hon. Secretary to whom all payments are to be made.

7. The Ambulance must not be used for infectious cases.

November, 1925.

The list of rules and regulations for the use of this the Red Cross motor ambulance service, formed in the 1920s, for local residents from November 1925. The ambulance was garaged at Bennett & Righton, one of Fareham's best-known motor traders.

old workhouse ended in 1967, when the piggeries were closed down.

Among the greatly feared killer diseases of earlier times were bronchitis and pneumonia. Bad as these were, local people tried to treat them at home with simple remedies from the pharmacy. Even more threatening were typhoid fever, diphtheria and scarlet fever because they frequently carried off young children. The isolation hospital in Highland Road cared for both children and adults suffering from these highly contagious diseases. The hospital, built in 1887, was enlarged in 1907. In 1891 44 patients were admitted and by 1901 the total number of admissions had risen to 130. These infectious cases possibly reflect the poor state of the town's cesspits and stagnant ditches at the latter end of the nineteenth century. Itinerant workers were thought to bring in contagious diseases; strawberry pickers, for example, were regularly inspected for signs of infectious illness which could threaten the community. It would be another 40 years before sewage disposal in Fareham and Portchester reached the required community health standard, although increased

The County Lunatic Asylum, as Knowle was originally known, opened in 1852. This aerial view, c.1925, illustrates the vast extent of the hospital 70 years later.

Knowle Hospital station, opened in May 1907, was at its busiest on Thursdays, which were visiting days for the hospital. This picture, c.1900, shows a man, thought to be Frank Pitt, on the steps of the signal box at Knowle which controlled the junction between the Meon Valley and Fareham to Eastleigh lines. The station closed in 1964, the signal box in 1973.

understanding of preventive measures and isolation of infectious patients helped save many lives.

It was 18 years after Queen Victoria came to the throne that the government passed the Pauper Lunatics Act. This was the culmination of a series of measures designed to deal with the problem of insane paupers. The process had begun in 1808 with the passing of the County Asylums Act, requiring local authorities to make proper provision for the

Nurses at Knowle Hospital, c.1900. Note the distinctive checked uniform beneath the copious aprons.

poor and mentally deficient in the community. Until this time the only provision for lunatics was to be found in the parish or union workhouses. In 1846 a committee of nine Justices of the Peace selected Knowle as the most suitable site for the erection of a lunatic asylum. The area comprised approximately 108 acres, which included a farm and the remains of a manor house. A purchase price of £5,500 was paid to the landowners and building began on 1 October 1851, the completion date being recorded as 1 June 1852. In the process millions of tons of bricks were supplied by the nearby Fontley Brickworks. At the end of the eight-month contract period, the total cost had reached £33,786. As well as the asylum for 400 inmates, the complex included an administrative centre, a residence for the medical superintendent and his family, a chapel, a laundry, a kitchen and separate wards for male and female inmates. Within a short time, Knowle acquired a farm and vegetable plots and its own small railway station, akin to the one at Netley Hospital. The County Lunatic Asylum, as Knowle was originally called, opened for admissions on 13 December 1852 and was at that time the second and the largest such institution to be built in the Wessex region. It was preceded by one built at Forston, in Dorset, a year or two earlier.

To the modern mind, the terms 'lunatic' and 'pauper', along with some of the comments in the early registers, are difficult to accept in this politically correct age. It should also be understood that the building of Knowle predated by nearly half a century the exploratory work and writings on the mind and personality by Sigmund Freud and other leading European psychoanalysts. In modern terms the rather harsh observations on Knowle's first patients simply echo a Victorian attempt at understanding these mentally ill and depressed people.

The first register of admissions makes compelling reading. There is also, just here and there, a hint of black humour in some of the entries. Patients came from a range of towns and villages across Hampshire. William Wrapson, appropriately from Fareham, is the first name to be recorded on the opening day. His mental disorder is monomania, a term which appears frequently in the first five years. Wrapson is described as in good health, although thin. He died in Knowle in 1876, his time there apparently almost a life sentence. Mary Ann Monday is recorded as the first female patient, 31 years old, a single woman and a Wickham labourer's daughter, suffering from dementia and described as 'thin and feeble and barely able to stand'. With the benefit of hindsight, it is perfectly possible to believe that many of these poor people were suffering from what we today would recognise as clinical depression, self-abuse, wife-beating and post-natal depression, all now treatable with drugs, counselling and psychotherapy. Two cases of obvious

Hants County Asylum, Fareham.

PARTICULARS OF NURSES PAY, EMOLUMENTS, LEAVE, etc.

Terms of Engagement — Nurses are engaged on one calendar month's probation, during which time they may leave or be discharged at any time. After probation they are fully engaged if satisfactory, and they then give or receive a calendar month's notice on leaving, except when summarily dismissed for misconduct.

Pay

SCALE OF PAY.	First Year £	Second Year £
Under Nurses	21	23*
Second Nurses	25	—
3rd and 4th Nurses (Infirmary Ward)	26	—
Second Nurses (Acute Wards L and B3, Epileptic Ward, M Ward & Idiot Block)	26	—
Second Nurse (Infirmary Ward)	29	—
Charge Nurses	32	—
Charge Nurse (H Ward)	34	—
Charge Nurses (Acute Wards L and B3, Epileptic Ward, M Ward, and Idiot Block)	36	—
Charge Nurse (Infirmary Ward)	38	—
Night Nurses	31	—
Second and Third Night Nurses	33	—
Charge Night Nurse	36	—

* This rise is conditional on the person proving competent and shewing a certain knowledge of her work.

Nurses who sing in the Choir receive £1 10s. per annum extra.

Nurses' wages are raised £3 per annum for good conduct on completion of five years' service, and again on completion of a further five years' service, with no subsequent increases.

£2 per annum is also given to holders of the Certificate of the Medico-Psychological Association, or to those who pass examination held by Superintendent.

Emoluments — Nurses have board (no beer), lodging, washing, and uniform, valued for the purpose of the Asylums Officers' Superannuation Act, 1909, at £30 per annum.

Superannuation. — Nurses are entitled to a Pension in accordance with the provisions of the Asylums Officers' Superannuation Act, 1909. For this purpose a deduction amounting to 3 per cent. per annum of the total value of the pay and emoluments is made in accordance with the Act.

In the case of anyone employed in an Asylum before 1st April, 1910 (Scotland 15th May, 1910), and who contracted out of the Asylums Officers' Superannuation Act, 1909, under Section 20, the wages will be £2 per annum less in all cases than that shewn in the above scale.

Travelling Expenses — Third Class rail fare (on taking up appointment) is paid after three months' service. (Trains stop at the Asylum Siding, Knowle platform.)

Leave

DAY NURSES:
1 day in 7.
14 days annual leave.
Every evening from 8 to 10 p.m., with the exception of about one evening a fortnight during the winter months.

NIGHT NURSES:
1 day in 7.
14 days annual leave.

An allowance of 15/- is given in lieu of rations whilst on Annual Leave and also an allowance at the rate of 3/4 per calendar month in lieu of dinner ration whilst on weekly leave. These cash allowances are included in value of emoluments as given above.

The above leave is granted conditionally to the requirements of the Asylum.

National Insurance — All the above employees are exempt from Part I. of the National Insurance Act, 1911, and therefore pay no contributions under the Act. A scheme prepared by the Visiting Committee, and approved by the Insurance Commissioners, is in force, providing sickness and disablement benefits, particulars of which, as applying to the above employees are given on the other side.

Medical Examination — In connection with the above every person entering the service of the Committee is required to undergo a medical examination as to physical fitness before being permanently appointed.

Duties — Nurses are engaged upon the express condition that they will act to the best of their power wherever and whenever their services may be required. Their duties comprise sick nursing, attending on the patients, seeing to their clothing, bedding, meals, employment and amusement, ward cleaning, and generally performing the duties usual in large Public Institutions.

1/4/14.

A leaflet giving details of nurses' pay and entitlements at Knowle in 1914. The details show the work was hard; the nurses only had one day off in seven, and a mere two hours' free time in the evenings. It was well worth joining the choir, however, for an additional 30s. a year!

post-natal depression are 19-year-old Anne Restell, suffering from puerperal mania, and 45-year-old Ann Williams, recently widowed and suffering from 'melancholia caused by confinement and childbirth'. She apparently quickly recovered and was discharged two months after admission. In some instances, Knowle patients were kept under observation. One example is that of Daniel Young, a boat builder from the Isle of Wight who was admitted on 3 April 1854 suffering from 'hallucination' and released two months later on a month's trial. Amy Grosvenor, 27, was admitted on 22 September 1854 suffering from melancholia due to her husband's absence in the Baltic. This being the period of the Crimean War, perhaps she feared being widowed without an income. Payments to the widows of soldiers were very small at this time.

Possibly a case of wife battering was that of Lydia Stone, suffering from acute mania and, while in good health, covered in bruises on her trunk and arms which she claimed were inflicted on her.

A labourer from the tanyard at Titchfield, 30-year-old George Gale is described as melancholic and suicidal. During two years at Knowle, Gale attempted suicide several times, once by opening a vein in his arm and losing four pints of blood in the process. By the summer of 1855 he had recovered and was released.

Some of the early patients took the matter of their release into their own hands. George Wildridge, a 34-year-old married carpenter entered Knowle in the summer of 1853 with 'acute mania but tolerable health'. Wildridge made several attempts at escape and finally succeeded six years later. He was not recaptured.

It is surprising to read that in 1854 the cigarette habit in patients was frowned upon. Agricultural labourer Brian Burn, 24, was admitted because of 'mania due to partial imbecility and inveterate smoking.' Some 50 years later, the annual report of 1903 observes:

The tendency is to send patients to Knowle for heavy drinking and smoking. Abstinence from alcohol and regular living soon make a wonderful difference to their mental state.

The National Health Service says much the same thing today.

Jane Bryde entered Knowle in November 1855 with 'religious delusions'. The surgeon wrote:

This patient died within twenty-four hours of her admission to the asylum of chronic gastritis. Her death was accelerated by a self-inflicted wound in her throat, one week prior to her admission.

Was this Knowle's way of denying responsibility for her death? We shall never know.

As we have seen, such terms as imbecile, lunatic, maniac and melancholic are widely used to describe these early patients. As late as 1891–1901 the census forms have descriptive columns headed 'deaf/dumb/blind/idiot/cripple', beneath which the enumerator could enter his comments as applicable.

Early medical treatment at Knowle was primitive and designed to restore the balance of what were known as the four vital humours: blood, phlegm, choler and melancholy. The type of simple drugs used to remove disorders by secretion were tincture, vesicans and spirits of aromatic ammonia. Expectorants helped remove phlegm and all these remedies were believed to restore the mental state affecting melancholia, mania, dementia and morality.

Knowle's first medical superintendent was Dr Ferguson and the matron was Mrs Hall. The working day began at 6a.m. with prayers followed by breakfast, after which the work attendants gathered up the able-bodied patients for work in the vegetable plots or the laundries. The non-working patients were raised from their beds and washed and dressed. The work of cleaning and supervising patients in the airing courts carried on throughout the day with short breaks for dinner and tea. Bedtime was at 8.30p.m. with lights out at 10p.m.

Knowle's farm and the vegetable plots, mainly worked by the patients, helped the hospital to be virtually self-sufficient as regards food. Meals were

A certificate awarded to Charge Nurse Eliza Jane Miles in March 1916. She had worked for 30 years at Knowle.

CARING FOR THE SICK

A happy group of nurses and some of their younger charges enjoy an alfresco tea party at Knowle, c.1930.

A prize-giving ceremony for student nurses at Knowle, c.1956.

The front elevation of Coldeast.

The back of Coldeast in the 1980s.

simple but healthy, in all probability better than those of the labouring poor in the local community. Knowle was able to keep the cost of caring for the patients low because so much of the work and many of the resources were in-house. In 1879 the weekly cost of keep for each patient was 9s.1¼d ! As to the pay of the staff in the very early years, the head attendant, shoemaker, tailor and gardener were each paid £25 per annum, while the foul-linen washer had to be content with £22.10s.

One thing is quite clear from the reports and registers. From its inception, Knowle made the well-being of the patients its main priority. For failing to do so, staff could be punished. In 1854, T. Charlick received a reprimand from the superintendent for putting a patient in a cold bath without permission. One nurse, V. Martin, was dismissed for using a cold bath on his ward as a punishment. Abusive nurses were severely dealt with: in 1899 a female nurse was summoned, convicted and dismissed for a violent assault on one of her patients.

Nurses who displayed neither interest in their charges nor tact in their management were given warnings. The remedy for this lack of enthusiasm was, however, a welcome one. In 1886 the management recommended a pay rise above £15 per annum. Thereafter, pay was reviewed regularly and small annual increments awarded.

The restraint and seclusion of sometimes violent patients came under review in 1888. The annual report showed that during the year five men and three woman had been under almost continuous restraint for a year, the men pinioned and the women with their hands tied behind their backs. The incoming superintendent, Dr Worthington, released these unfortunates and greatly reduced the isolation of the most violent patients.

By the early-twentieth century, the acquisition of further buildings and training of staff in the by now recognised field of psychiatric medicine continued. Salaries and conditions of work improved. By 1953, nurses' pay was £513 per annum with four weeks' annual leave.

By the time Knowle came under the administration of the National Health Service, the hospital could offer the full range of psychiatric care and medicine, unimaginable to the original staff of 1852. Its closure in 1992 marked the end of 150 years of service to the mentally sick of Hampshire. Today, only Ravenswood House, managed by the local NHS Trust, remains on the vastly redeveloped site that once was Knowle.

Other aspects of the mental health of the community were addressed in the 1920s, when Hampshire County Council purchased the Coldeast estate. The house itself was built early in the nineteenth century, when it was the home of Admiral Sir Samuel Hood. At his death it was owned by Quintin Hogg, philanthropist and founder of the Regent Street Polytechnic in London, who sold it to the Montefiore family.

Coldeast's first designation was as a colony for the mentally deficient. The principle behind this establishment was the need to keep mentally frail adults living together with their children under the care and supervision of professional staff. By so doing, it was envisaged that these people, with the help and guidance of trained staff, would be able to lead relatively independent lives.

During the Second World War, part of the site was taken over by the government as an emergency hospital in the event of heavy bombing in the Fareham region.

After 1948, the colony at Coldeast became a mental hospital. Changes in recent years have meant that the work of the hospital carries on today in separate units on the original site.

✤ CHAPTER 12 ✤

Fareham and the Second World War

In an interview for the *Portsmouth Evening News* in the closing weeks of the war, Mrs F. Dyke, Chairman of Fareham Urban District Council, offered her hopes for the town after the depredations of the war. This would be a look to the future and a chance to bring the old rural Fareham and its numerous villages forward into the twentieth century. But first came the war years. How did Fareham cope?

Unlike Portsmouth and Gosport, Fareham had no large military establishments producing weapons and building and repairing ships. It did, however, have the vulnerability of a community strategically placed between the cities of Portsmouth and Southampton. The fear of Luftwaffe planes jettisoning bombs was a real one. For example, several high-explosive bombs landed on the villages of Droxford, Meonstoke and Soberton, which were among the chosen evacuation places for children from Portsmouth and Gosport.

There was, however one military establishment which differed from others in the harbour area. HMS Collingwood became operational on 10 January 1940 as a New Entry Training Establishment for Hostilities Only for the Seaman Branch. A year earlier, 197 acres of unpromising marshland south of Fort Fareham had been purchased for £7,290. According to the landowner, the site was the finest piece of cornland in the whole of Southern England. Locals had other views. They regarded it as the best snipe marsh in the county, ideal for the sportsman with an eye to the main chance. It was so wet and boggy that sea-boots were a necessary part of one's attire when straying

A portrait of Admiral Lord Collingwood, 1750–1810.

Dan the terrier dog mascot with officers of the newly-commissioned HMS Collingwood on 10 January 1940.

99

'Ten weeks in the life of a recruit'. Four men from different walks of life in the various stages of training, from their arrival at HMS Collingwood to readiness for the Senior Service after two and a half months.

FAREHAM AND THE SECOND WORLD WAR

The ceremony of hoisting the colours at HMS Collingwood, 13 July 1943. The parade ground at this time was the largest in Europe.

The officers' mess at HMS Collingwood, suitably dressed up for a ladies' night during the Second World War.

King George VI emerging from a shelter at HMS Collingwood, 25 July 1940.

off the few footpaths. When work began on site, large concrete rafts were put into position to stabilise each building. It would be the 1950s before any substantial two-storeyed buildings could be erected on this former swamp.

Fareham's HMS Collingwood was the fourth to bear this illustrious title. Named after Lord Cuthbert Collingwood, Nelson's second-in-command at Trafalgar, there were three earlier ships bearing the same name launched in 1841, 1887 and 1908 respectively. In this vast new Fareham establishment, groups of up 1,000 men arrived every three weeks to undergo a range of training courses. Its medical section was rated as a naval hospital and the parade ground was the largest in Europe. The first Wren to arrive was the daughter of an admiral. As she brought the family's portable typewriter with her by bicycle from Alverstoke, she was promptly appointed assistant secretary to Commodore C.G. Sedgwick, Collingwood's commanding officer. During January of 1940 a further 50 Wrens arrived, all initially untrained but eventually serving as messengers, telephonists, stewards and cooks.

Collingwood sustained several bombing raids. On 18 June 1943, 30 Wrens were killed, all of whom are buried in a communal grave in Portsmouth. Ceremonial divisions were suspended throughout Portsmouth Command after bomb damage at Collingwood in 1941 resulted in a number of casualties to the men on parade.

An earlier air-raid alert caught George VI unawares. On a visit to the establishment when the raid occurred in 1940, he took shelter with the men. The autographed photograph of the smiling king emerging from the shelter is a prized memento of the war years at HMS Collingwood.

In 1938 the Fareham Urban District Council had responded to the government's Air Raid Precaution Act by delivering Anderson shelters to Fareham residents. These simple devices would prove to be life-savers for thousands of people in residential areas. The then Home Secretary, Sir John Anderson, gave his name to this 6ft by 4½ft kennel-shaped construction of six curved and corrugated steel sheets bolted together at the top to form an arch. When covered with earth the finished article looked not unlike a brown igloo. The shelters were supplied free of charge to those families earning less than £250 per annum – an average lower-middle-class income in 1939. Those families above this limit could buy a shelter for £7 plus the cost of erection. Where there was a shortage of able-bodied men in the home, local authority workmen, public-spirited wardens or, occasionally, Boy Scouts helped dig the deep hole

FAREHAM AND THE SECOND WORLD WAR

A group of German prisoners of war at Camp 251, Fareham. The camp was located between Downend Road and the railway line; after the war the former prison huts were used as temporary accommodation for the homeless.

needed to accommodate the shelter. Elsewhere, public shelters made of reinforced brick and concrete sprang up at strategic points. Ten of these were built in Fareham, nine in the immediate vicinity of West Street and one in High Street near the Golden Lion public house. The surrounding villages were not forgotten. At Portchester, a shelter capable of taking 500 people was erected at Newtown, while Sarisbury and Titchfield had two apiece.

The responsibility for the management of these public shelters lay with the ARP, based from 1939 in offices in Portland Chambers, close to the bus station. Rules were laid down as to the correct behaviour required in public shelters. It was an offence for a person to enter or remain in a shelter 'if he is drunk or if his person or clothing is offensively unclean or verminous.' He must not:

> *... by forcible or improper means enter or seek to enter any sanitary convenience in or appurtenant to the shelter or knowingly intrude upon the privacy of a person using such a convenience.*

These rather pompous regulations make amusing reading today but it was often the case that derelicts would set up home in the shelters, leaving them littered with broken bottles, abandoned food and cigarette butts.

ARP wardens, both male and female, appeared everywhere when needed and generally inspired confidence in the local populace, though they had their limitations.

On 20 September 1940 the following notice appeared on the notice board of the Portchester wardens' HQ:

> *To all group wardens – Childbirth During Air Raids. Should enquiries for assistance be made to Wardens it is recommended that they get in touch with the nearest midwife or doctor. Do not contact the first aid post unless no other assistance is possible.*
> *Resident midwives – Nurse Dicker, 5 Mountview Avenue; Nurse Grundy, 10 Windsor Road; Mrs Wallis, 152 White Hart Lane.*

This is well before the days of the ubiquitous paramedic!

Young families, the sick and the disabled could apply to have another form of shelter installed inside the house. This was the Morrison shelter, named after Herbert Morrison, Home Office Minister at the time. It was, in effect, a long steel table, about 6½ft long, 4ft wide and 2½ft high with mesh sides. During the day it served as the family's dining table while at night it could, at a pinch, accommodate two adults and two small children and even, occasionally, the family pets.

Surprisingly, Fareham children, unlike the children of neighbouring towns, were not evacuated. Thus the responsibility for the care and protection of

Four prisoners at the door of their hut in Camp 251. It is possible that the men imprisoned here at this time were among those who helped lay out and build the Bridgemary housing estate at the end of the war.

schoolchildren when outside the home rested fairly and squarely with their teachers. It was essential also to keep up the morale of their young charges. Fortunately, humour kept breaking through. On one occasion a harassed young teacher from Redlands Lane Junior School was escorting her crocodile of children to the Tin Tabernacle in Mill Road, in use as an overspill classroom, when a passer-by enquired, 'Are those children all yours?' 'Yes, all mine but with different fathers,' came the reply.

At the outset of the war, Fareham Urban District Council had distributed to all residents a booklet entitled *What(s) to do*. This publication listed all the rest centres available in the event of heavy bombing raids. These included the Harrison Road Senior School, which could accommodate 200 people. Portchester had rest centres at the Methodist Sunday School and the Junior School in Castle Street, with much larger accommodation at the Senior School in White Hart Lane.

An administrative centre was set up in the Foresters' Hall, where local residents could go for information, particularly after heavy raids. Casualty lists were also posted outside Westbury Manor. The Foresters' Hall simultaneously doubled as the town's Food Office where, among other nutritional benefits, mothers could obtain precious bottles of orange juice from America, which boosted the Vitamin C content of their children's diets. At No. 86 West Street, donations of clothing and kitchen equipment were distributed to the victims of bombing by the Women's

Some of the prisoners added their signatures to this drawing of Hut 26, made by an inmate at Camp 251.

FAREHAM AND THE SECOND WORLD WAR

Bomb damage in Colenso Road, March 1941.

Colenso Road, March 1941. Residents of the area look on in bewilderment at the damage.

Voluntary Service. These redoubtable women were not merely jam-makers; as the war drew to a close they were involved in a number of specialised procedures, including the decontamination of clothing belonging to German prisoners of war and assisting in the interrogation of these men.

After particularly heavy raids, such as in 1943 when a huge landmine fell on Portchester's Cornerway Lane killing several people, the morning air was permeated with the smoke from anti-aircraft guns. Much of the devastation caused by such bombing raids was untouched for several years. For local children, the aftermath of the raids provided a new and fascinating hobby. The collection of pieces of shrapnel was enjoyed by large numbers of children who vied with friends for the largest amount and the biggest individual specimen. One Fareham boy recalled that his own hoard included the tail fin of a German bomb complete with the manufacturer's markings!

Fareham children, by all accounts, took a keen interest in the war on their doorsteps. One small Fareham girl was reported as being so ARP-minded she spent some time blacking out her doll's house with pieces of wood and shoring up some of its rooms. Adults at this time would have been fitting out the family home with heavy blackout curtains and sticky-taping the windows against the expected bomb blast damage. Fareham's boys were proud of their expertise at plane-spotting. The local paper reported that many of them insisted they could

Farmers were encouraged to 'Plough for Victory' during the war, and here a local farmer is accompanied on his tractor by three landgirls. A large crowd lines West Street to applaud their appearance which was part of a patriotic procession through the town.

Members of the Royal Air Force parade behind the band along West Street during 'Wings for Victory' week, 10–17 April 1943. This was just one of many campaigns during the war to raise both morale and funds.

❖ FAREHAM AND THE SECOND WORLD WAR ❖

A parade of policemen, followed by local firemen, march past officials and schoolchildren near the old Post Office in West Street during the Second World War.

distinguish between the types of aircraft, even those flying at a great height.

Although Fareham and its villages suffered more lightly than either Portsmouth or Gosport, it had its fair share of raids. In the period between June 1940 and November 1944 there were over 1,500 alerts, with 22 people killed outright or fatally wounded. A further 59 needed hospital treatment and 119 suffered minor injuries. Of Fareham's pre-war housing stock, 79 homes were totally destroyed and 165 rendered uninhabitable, while a further 4,000 underwent emergency repairs.

One interesting innovation was the institution of British Restaurants. A brainchild of the Ministry of Food, these were devised to ensure that essential workers in particular, as well as service men and women, had access to cheap, nourishing food. The midday meal was initially priced at 10d., puddings were 2d., egg and chips 8d. and tea and coffee 1½d. a cup. A cash-and-carry system offered take-away meals at the same prices. Fareham's first British Restaurant opened off Westbury Road, followed by another at West Street, Portchester. While it was undoubtedly true that many workers were appreciative of the ready availability of cheap, hot food, the restaurants came in for fierce criticism both for the standard of cooking and the size of helpings.

The war had its lighter moments. On the farms of Fareham and in its villages, members of the Women's Land Army were a familiar and cheerful sight. The whole nation was engaged in the mighty effort to produce meat, fruit and vegetables to supplement the rather dull minimum food ration. Such large institutions as HMS Collingwood were no exception. The staff had their own piggery and masses of vegetables and fruit were cultivated. Fareham schoolchildren helped out by picking blackberries and rosehips during the hot August days. It was remarkable that the seasons were so sharply defined during the 1940s. The winters were bitterly cold, especially that of 1946/7, while summers were long, hot and sunny.

How to keep up the morale of the people was a subject of concern to the government. One solution was the Holidays at Home scheme, inaugurated in 1942. The principal object of the exercise was to discourage people from travelling too far from home at a time when fuel for public transport was in desperately short supply. Equally important was the need to entertain people by organising various events, particularly sporting and musical, within their own community. Fareham, in common with other towns up and down the land, obliged. A surviving Holidays at Home programme for 1943 affords a delightful view of the innocent (by today's standards) pastimes devised for the people of Fareham in August of that year. Sports enthusiasts

Residents of Red Barn Lane prepare to enjoy their VE Day party in May 1945.

were catered for with a grand boxing tournament at the Connaught Hall, while at Bath Lane recreation ground the Hampshire Constabulary fielded a cricket team against the Portsmouth City Police. Wallington residents enjoyed a grand fête with a Punch and Judy show and no less than three beauty competitions, Bathing Belle, Best Coiffeur and Best Ankle – the latter having an almost Victorian feel. There were bandaging competitions fiercely contested by such voluntary organisations as the St John Ambulance. Music lovers heard opera singer Robert Easton at a celebrity concert at the Methodist Hall, King's Road. Throughout the month there were grand dances and cabarets, while a mobile cinema parked at Bath Lane recreation ground showed continuous morale-building films on the progress of the war. Proceeds from many of these events went to war charities.

By the spring of 1944 the people of Fareham were aware that momentous events were afoot. A large influx of British and Commonwealth troops started moving through the town on their way to the forward assembly areas prior to D-Day. As one man, a schoolboy at the time, recalls:

We lived in Wallington and there were about 50 tanks parked by the big, posh houses' lawns near our school, by St Peter and St Paul Church.

One of the assembly points was the vast, wooded acreage of Cams Hall, then being used by a Portsmouth Dockyard department. A woman who worked there as a tracer remembers the Marine encampment in the fields beside the main drive up to the hall. On 6 June, the Head of Staff brought his wireless into the office and allowed the girls to listen to the first reports of the landings broadcast by the BBC.

FAREHAM AND THE SECOND WORLD WAR

Party hats and fancy dress marked the occasion at this VE Day party at the Hoeford Inn in May 1945.

Between October 1943 and May 1944, the Gosport and Fareham Omnibus Co. regularly conveyed thousands of special workmen to and from Stokes Bay, where 14 of the massive concrete walls of the Mulberry Harbours were constructed.

In common with other communities throughout the United Kingdom, Fareham celebrated the peace with sing-songs, flags and street parties. On Sunday 13 May 1945, a special thanksgiving service for the cessation of hostilities in Europe was held at Holy Trinity Church, conducted by the vicar, the Revd B.C. Daniell and the Revd A.C. Eastman, President of the Free Churches Council. It was, perhaps, entirely appropriate that one of the hymns was 'Praise My Soul the King of Heaven', composed by Fareham's Sir John Goss, organist for many years at St Paul's Cathedral and a favourite of Queen Victoria.

The chapter began with Mrs F. Dyke's aspirations for post-war Fareham. Necessity is often said to be the mother of invention and, like so many other towns throughout the land, at the end of the Second World War, Fareham was, in many senses, obliged to make a new beginning. Mrs Dyke's first priority was the construction of new homes. She proposed the erection of 100 temporary homes, the much-loved 'pre-fabs', which would prove to be anything but temporary. A further 200 permanent homes would be built in the Fareham Ward and a further 50 each in Sarisbury and Titchfield.

Today, it seems hard to believe that in the 1930s Portchester had few made-up roads, while its sewerage system left much to be desired. On a happier note, post-war Portchester would also get its own cinema. Mrs Dyke envisaged a public library, a maternity home and a large public car park, as well as a civic centre, which she regarded as essential. By far the biggest scheme, however, was that for the Mill Pond at Cams, described as a major redevelopment. This would comprise a golf links, ornamental gardens, a swimming pool, a boating lake and a children's paddling pool. The entire council believed this project would provide attractions for visitors and residents alike.

Mrs Dyke's interview for the *Evening News* ended on an ominous note; no plans had been finalised for Fareham's future improvements and the council had no idea as to the cost of the various projects outlined!

The war was the catalyst for the new, much larger Fareham but it would be another 30 years before many of Mrs Dyke's aspirations became a reality.

Tributes to the memory of the fallen of two world wars provide a moving sight at the War Memorial outside Holy Trinity Church in November 2005. Inset: The thanksgiving service for the end of the war was held at Holy Trinity Church on 13 May 1945.

CHAPTER 13

Childhood Memories of Portchester and Fareham – by Pam Webb

My earliest memories of Portchester are from about 1938 when I was three years old. Opposite our bungalow on the A27 was a beautiful field of corn and on the edge of the field next to the road was a huge advertising hoarding which was illuminated at night. I was not to see that lit up again for six years, and the field of corn was to become allotments. Just as war was declared in 1939, my father was away at his TA Army Camp. He sent a message to say he would have to go straight to the call-up depot, but he would be on the train passing through Portchester. My grandparents, my mother and I went up to the railway fence behind The Crossways and waved to him as he went by. I can remember very clearly standing on a farm gate, which must have been at a crossing point for cattle, and seeing him waving out of the train window. Except for the odd leave, I was not to see him again for six years.

The war years seemed to be continuously long hot summers and very cold winters with my mother and grandmother either frantically bottling fruit and making jam or piling on extra woollies to keep warm. My grandparents lived in a bungalow next door and our gardens were combined at the back, so we were able to grow all our own fruit and vegetables right through the war. There was frantic making of blackout frames for the windows and the sticking of yards of brown paper strips across them in case of blast damage. The Anderson shelter arrived and I had to give up my special bit of garden and my swing to make space for it. Most children had what we called 'siren suits' to wear to the shelter at night: warm trousers, a jersey and a pixie hood. Unfortunately one winter our Anderson filled with water and as a result I caught pneumonia so then we had a Morrison table shelter indoors. This was a very strong iron table with wire-mesh sides and mattresses to lie on. It was quite a squeeze when we all got under the table shelter: my grandmother and her dog, a large fat Aberdeen terrier, my mother and I and my grandfather, who was almost six feet tall. You could just about sit up, underneath, but it was more comfortable lying down. Although we didn't use the Anderson for very long, I shall never forget the smell of the garden on summer nights when the 'all clear' sounded and my grandfather carried me indoors again to my bed. It must have been a mixture of damp earth and smoke from the anti-aircraft guns because in the morning we used to go round with a bucket picking up the shrapnel on the grass.

Portchester was quite heavily bombed throughout the war, probably due to the near misses from the top end of

The Castle, Portchester, one of the finest examples of a Roman fortification in Britain. The keep is a later construction, from Norman times.

This aerial photograph gives a good impression of the grandeur of the Portchester Castle site. St Mary's Church can be seen in the right foreground.

the harbour and dockyard, as a great many ships were anchored in the upper reaches of the creeks, and the German bombers would also have been aiming for the railway line. They also dropped their surplus bombs in the mud on their way home and in the morning there was often mud on the roads and roofs of the houses. Later in the war, Portchester had a very bad night. It must have been 1943 as I had just started my new school. Where the Seagull public house is now, at Cornerway Lane, a bomb from the previous nights raid had exploded, leaving the largest hole I have ever seen; it was years before the hole was filled in. Several people were killed in The Crossways, and that particular night our back door blew off and the dining-room windows were smashed in on top of the Morrison shelter. The gas was cut off and in the morning my mother turned our little electric fire onto its back and boiled the kettle on it to make a cup of tea. Lying in bed at night I could hear the trains on the railway line; sometimes the sound of the goods trains went on and on through the night. I now realise this must have been the build-up to D-Day. Earlier in the war, the night Portsmouth was badly fire-bombed, my grandfather was on fire duty in Portchester, and he saw the glow in the sky over Portsmouth and feared the Guildhall had been hit. He came to tell us, almost in tears, because he was in charge of the Food Office in Portsmouth and he did, in fact, lose all the records and had to start again in Mayfield Road School, in North End.

During the long hot summers when we were not making jam or bottling fruit, my mother and I used to walk. As the proper beaches were all out of bounds during the war, we made do with the creeks around Portchester Castle. I did all my paddling on the muddy flint and seaweed-covered beaches, always hoping to find a Roman coin, but never being successful. We often took my friend with us and our favourite walk was down Castle Street to Cow Lane and then across the water-meadows and what was left of the medieval maltings. From there you could look northwards across the upper reaches of the harbour to Portsdown Hill, and westwards to the backs of the long gardens of the very old houses and cottages in Castle Street. We came up through the Iron-Age ditch to the Castle, just by the Land Gate. If the weather was good and we didn't need the shelter of the Castle walls, we went out through the Water Gate and turned right and walked round to the Urchins Meadow, usually full of cows, and sat under the sea-wall. We had a picnic of things like jam or chocolate spread sandwiches and my friend and I would share a bottle of Tizer lemonade, and my mother would usually have a flask of tea. Sometimes we went home a different way along Wicor Path, so called as it once led to Wicor Mill, by then long gone. On its was site a bone factory that made glue. The smell was dreadful and we always knew when it was going to rain as the west wind blew the smell across Portchester.

CHILDHOOD MEMORIES OF PORTCHESTER AND FAREHAM

Hunting and beagling was quite popular among the upper classes in this area at the start of the twentieth century. These elegant huntsmen are both Portchester gentlemen.

This path to Wicor was still through fields and open ground during the war and we cut across White Hart Lane and went along Chalky Path (it really was beaten-down chalk) and out onto the A27, just opposite the end of the Downsway. If we came back up Castle Street we would pass the dairy opposite the White Hart pub, where our milk came from. The cows were kept on the water-meadows at the back of Castle Street.

One day, a strange-looking vehicle drew up opposite our bungalow. It had a large chimney on a trailer and it was for making smoke when there was an air-raid on, so as to confuse the bombers. We called them Smokey-Joes! They didn't last very long; I don't think they were very successful. The next thing we had, just along the road, where there had been cornfields right up to Cornerway Lane, was a barrage balloon site. This lasted a lot longer than the Smokey-Joes. Then, later in the war, we had some American soldiers stationed on the site; it would have been during the build-up to D-Day. One day, there was a knock at the door and a young black American stood there offering us a tin of pineapple. I don't think my mother had ever seen a black person except at the cinema, but we thought the pineapple was manna from heaven. Food was a problem and usually my grandmother looked after me and my mother queued up for the special things that were off ration, like fish and rabbit. My grandmother was very fond of rabbit, although my mother wouldn't touch it. I used to sneak in next door and have some rabbit stew and dumplings or rabbit pie, whenever I could. One of the things I really liked was an omelette made with dried egg, and another was Spam. A friend across the road kept chickens and ducks and sometimes my grandfather had a duck egg as a treat. I was very taken with the lovely pale duck-egg blue of its shell.

At the end of the war we had the V1s. They were rockets and really scary. When you heard the drone of the engine stop you knew it was about to come down, and we used to count, rather like people do between lightning and thunder, to see how far away it is, only this wasn't for fun – it was real. Then at last came victory! We had the usual street party and rejoicing. The blackout curtains came down and the brown paper came off the windows, the Anderson shelter went, and I had my own piece of garden once again.

After the excitement of my father coming home, with his trunk full of oranges and pomegranates from Gibraltar, where he had been for the last four years of the war, life continued; rationing continued and things were still in short supply. Portchester remained much as it had been in 1939, apart from the bomb damage, until the 1950s when the housing development really got under way. The west side of Cornerway Lane was still a country hedge and fields stretched all the way to Cams Hall (apart from the smallholdings and Birdwood Grove). The allotments opposite our bungalow returned to growing corn and the hoarding was repainted and illuminated once again. My friend and I, older now, were allowed to go for walks on our own. Our favourite one was to Upper Cornerway Lane railway bridge (the original one) where we could listen for the whistle of a train pulling away from Portchester Station. We waited on the bridge for the smoke and steam to surround us completely; it was like being in the clouds. We would continue up the lane, the fields of Red Barn Farm on either side, to a sharp left turn and in a field next to the hedge was an old railway carriage in which lived a tramp. This lane was always known as 'Old Man's Lane', whether because of this tramp I never knew. The other walk we liked was up to the top of Station Road to the old chalk pit (the original one, first dug by the Romans when they built Portchester Castle) then straight on up over the grassy slope to the road at the top of the hill. This grassy path was called Monk's Walk; it was the way the monks came down from Southwick to visit the church in the Castle grounds after they had moved their priory from there up to Southwick. There were still lovely wild flowers on the hill then: harebells, orchids, lady's slippers and

Mrs F. Dyke opening the Portchester Allotment Show in 1951. Mrs Dyke was a prominent member of Fareham Urban District Council for many years, and was also the local organiser of the Women's Voluntary Service.

The children of the junior school at Wicor celebrate the coronation of Queen Elizabeth II in 1953.

CHILDHOOD MEMORIES OF PORTCHESTER AND FAREHAM

The Savoy Buildings were built in the 1930s, replacing a group of older houses and trees. Here is the parade in the 1950s, with Woolworth's prominent in the centre. The larger building towards the centre of the picture is the Embassy Cinema, with the Victor Value supermarket next door.

hundreds more. During the spring the larks sang all day above the hill.

Two places stick in my mind in the village that were still there in the late 1940s, the blacksmith and the clay pipe factory. The blacksmith was on the south side of East Street, just past the crossroads, and the pipe factory, owned by the firm of Leigh, was just inside Castle Street. As clay pipes had long gone, the factory made putty and lime products. The wall adjoining Castle Street was slatted wood and you could peep through the slats at the men working within and smell the chalky material. There was still a village policeman who lived in the police house, and a chimney sweep who cycled around on his bike with his face all black. Alas, those days are long gone and Portchester is a different place now. Yet in the odd corner and down near the Castle, you can still see and feel echoes of the past.

My most enduring memory is of being met by my mother outside my school, which was Wykeham House, in the High Street and being taken to the cinema. As school finished at 3.30p.m., there was plenty of time to visit the café at the Savoy Cinema before seeing the film. Decorated in Art Deco style and with french-windows and a balcony, I thought it was wonderfully 'grown-up'. Because of the time, we always saw the 'big' picture first, and if we didn't like the 'second' picture we just left and went home. Once there was a practice air-raid and tear gas was used and we had to sit and watch the film wearing our gas-masks. Being right opposite the bus station it wasn't far to go for the bus. Sometimes we went to the Embassy, which wasn't quite as exciting as there was no cafe.

I expect everyone remembers that lovely shop Letherens and the overhead rail network that ran to the cashier's office. Absolutely fascinating, watching the little wooden pots whizzing along the wires and then returning with the change. A more upmarket shop was Philip's, where they sold, amongst other things, very posh hats. Woolworth's was a good mecca to head for. If you were lucky, you might just catch a consignment of pencils, rubbers and notebooks, all of which were in short supply in the war years. Later on, when we were a little older, the L-shape of Woolworth's was useful to meet the boys from Price's School, amongst the gardening tools and household items and out of view of the rest of the shop.

Another interesting place was Pyle's, a cake shop and restaurant. Very occasionally, I had lunch there as a change from school dinners. The shop always smelled of sweet cakes and icing sugar. We were on our honour to go straight back to school after having lunch, but some of the more daring girls stayed out and met the boys from Price's.

During the school holidays, a favourite pastime was to go to Fareham's market. Market day was Monday and it really was a proper market with all the usual farm animals and sometimes rabbits and chickens as well. My friend and I loved watching the cattle being unloaded from the huge cattle trucks to go into the compound and then listen to the auctioneer selling them, not a word of which we could understand! At certain times of the year there were sheep. They would try to jump out of their pens and it was great fun when one did succeed.

I remember the 'big freeze' of the winter of 1946/7 and the huge lumps of ice on the creek at Wallington; the mill pond side was solid with just a few tufts of seagrass showing above the snow-covered ice and the River Wallington barely a trickle under the ice, coming out under the A27 bridge. Up until this time Fareham was still very rural and it felt as if you lived in the country and then the post-war development began and changed Fareham for ever.

One of the many interesting things about the topography of Fareham before this development were the many footpaths and alleys that criss-crossed the town from east to west, with others coming up from the West Street. These probably marked the boundaries of fields and footpaths from medieval times. The whole area now covered by the shopping precinct was allotments, crossed by Westbury Lane, Pyle's Alley and Hobbs's garage. The footpath that ran along at the rear of Southampton Road was especially interesting as it could be followed from west to east from Park Lane to the Wallington River and came out at Bridgefoot by the old A27, by the viaduct.

A pleasant scene alongside the River Wallington in 1983. The river and much of the creek was frozen over in the harsh winter of 1946/7.

An aerial view of Fareham High Street and surrounds, c.1930. Note the Parish Church (top left). Church Path (often known as Pyle's Alley because it met West Street next to the bakery of that name) runs down the left-hand side past the allotments and long gardens of the houses. Wallington Hill is the road that turns right off High Street at the top, and Wallington Shore Road winds its way alongside the river (top right). Much of the pleasant greenery to the right of High Street has since been rudely disturbed by the traffic artery known as Wallington Way.

✧ CHAPTER 14 ✧

The Buildings of Fareham

Lysses House Hotel, an impressive Georgian building which served both as a house and as a private school. Its sense of spacious elegance has been maintained to this day.

It surely would be true to say that Fareham has a range of buildings of unusual interest and design. It is almost certainly the case that the buildings themselves are important for what they tell us about the people who built them and those who lived in them. Fareham's buildings are not spectacular or grandiose. The best of them sit comfortably in tune with the local ambience. For many years High Street has enjoyed the plaudits of architectural historians and has been described as the best preserved Georgian street in Hampshire. This is, in fact, something of a misnomer as behind many of the elegant eighteenth-century façades there lurk constructions of a much earlier date and style. Probably the best example of this is No. 15 on the western side, once known as 'Chives', a very popular restaurant during the 1970s and 1980s. This fascinating building has several levels and numerous small staircases. Researchers over the past decade have dated the building to the late-thirteenth century. Some 200 years ago the street was the favoured residence of naval officers and their families. In more recent times, No. 70 Kintyre House was the home of Admiral Leonard Donaldson who, between the wars, was a councillor on Fareham Urban District Council. Wykeham House School was next door and girls at the school during the 1940s may remember the admiral's reported irritation with the stray balls that were frequently lobbed over the wall into his beautiful garden! Kintyre House retains its classical eighteenth-century elevation and pillared entrance, as do others in High Street. There was never any 'trade' here; it was exclusively the domain of wealthy and discerning citizens.

For centuries, West Street has been the trading centre of Fareham, the width of the street telling us that this was an important market town. On both the north and south sides there remain a number of interesting and historical buildings. The Red Lion Hotel is a reminder of Fareham's past as a staging post for coaches carrying passengers and mail beyond the town to the outside world, while the magnificent pillared façade of the Warner Goodman Street building housed Portland Hall. This was the home of the Society for Literary and Philosophical Objects, and is an echo of a more gracious age. Perhaps the naval officers and their families left the seclusion of High Street to attend elegant meetings here.

The lower end of High Street c.1920. **On the far left, May's garage, formerly a cycle works, now has a petrol pump to cater for the new motorists. Edney's, the corn and seed merchant, can be seen on the opposite corner.**

This photograph was taken in 2003 from almost the same location. All the buildings are still in place; Abraham's the upholsterers, next to the garage in the previous picture, has now become Hansford's fishing-tackle shop, but still retains its first floor wrought-iron balcony railings.

THE BUILDINGS OF FAREHAM

High Street in 1981, showing a fine group of buildings including the former 'Chives' restaurant (in the centre), which, like so many other buildings in the street, is much older than it appears at first glance, and probably originally dates from the thirteenth century. Note the fine lamppost – there are many of this type in High Street, erected in honour of Queen Victoria's diamond jubilee in 1897.

Groups of houses on the north-eastern side of High Street. Buildings such as these reflect the elegant period of the eighteenth and nineteenth centuries, when this area of Fareham was a favourite residence for wealthy naval officers in particular. The building on the right with the tall chimneys was once a single large medieval house, but was converted into three cottages in Georgian days.

Once Wykeham House School, No. 69 High Street was originally built of red brick. It was refaced in the early nineteenth century by the then fashionable process of 'mathematical tiling', giving it a yellowish appearance.

The north side of West Street has suffered casualties over the years. Two of these were the Savoy and Embassy cinemas, both attractive examples of the Art Deco style of architecture and design. Many older local residents will have fond memories of these two 'picture palaces' – their first date, perhaps, or queuing up in wartime Fareham to see their favourite Hollywood movie star.

Opposite the Savoy on the south side is Westbury Manor Museum, arguably one of the very best of Hampshire's local museums. The building began life as a seventeenth-century farmhouse and in the eighteenth and early-nineteenth centuries was home to a succession of admirals of the Royal Navy. Here is an 1810 description of Westbury Manor:

Messuage and tenement, coachhouse and stables, other offices and garden belonging to the late Vice Admiral Thomas Alexander, and situate on the south side of West Street.

Appropriately, the walls and stairway once held

The Red Lion Hotel, seen here in the 1980s from the corner of High Street, was once a staging post for coaches. Although the interior has seen many changes over the years, the façade is an elegant reminder of Fareham's more leisurely days.

THE BUILDINGS OF FAREHAM

A drawing by B.J. Robertson of Fareham Town Quay in 1989. Originally the town's sea trading centre, it is now a conservation area where some of the attractive older buildings have been renovated for domestic and other uses.

portraits of all the admirals who had lived here. Happily, Westbury Manor is still just recognisable from this 200-year-old description, but a big chunk of the splendid garden was lost in 1953 to make way for the Hants & Dorset Co. bus station. The Hampshire broadcaster and journalist John Arlott wrote that West Street was once a leafy thoroughfare and that the presence of Westbury Manor was a reminder of the street's civilised and gracious past.

The last private owners of the manor sold it to Fareham Urban District Council in 1932 for £3,500 as the town's venue for civic and municipal business and thus it remained until 1976, when the new civic offices were completed. The extensions at the rear of the building were demolished in the 1970s, breaking the link with the Second World War, when they housed the town's Air Raid Control Centre.

Debates then raged as to the fate of the now fast-deteriorating building. Throughout the region, an enthusiasm for local history and museums grew as people began to realise that with so much change this, maybe, was the moment to recapture Fareham's past and reinterpret it for future citizens and local historians. Westbury Manor was considered a likely candidate, but not before another house, No. 29 Wickham Road, was bequeathed to the town by Miss Winifred Cocks in her will for use as a museum or some other charitable trust. Fareham people have always enjoyed a good argument about their town's future. In respect of a possible museum, the pros and the antis put forward their cases. The affair was settled in favour of Westbury Manor when, in 1985, Hampshire County Council offered a grant of £300,000 for its restoration, matching funding to be supplied by Fareham Borough Council. As a consequence, Westbury Manor Museum flourishes today, one good reason surely being that it faces the main shopping thoroughfare, making it accessible to those who wish to drop in as they go about their daily business. The more remote Wickham Road location would have been unlikely to attract these visitors.

At Lower Quay, a number of the buildings remind us of Fareham's maritime past. The Rope House, Chandlery and Customs House have all been

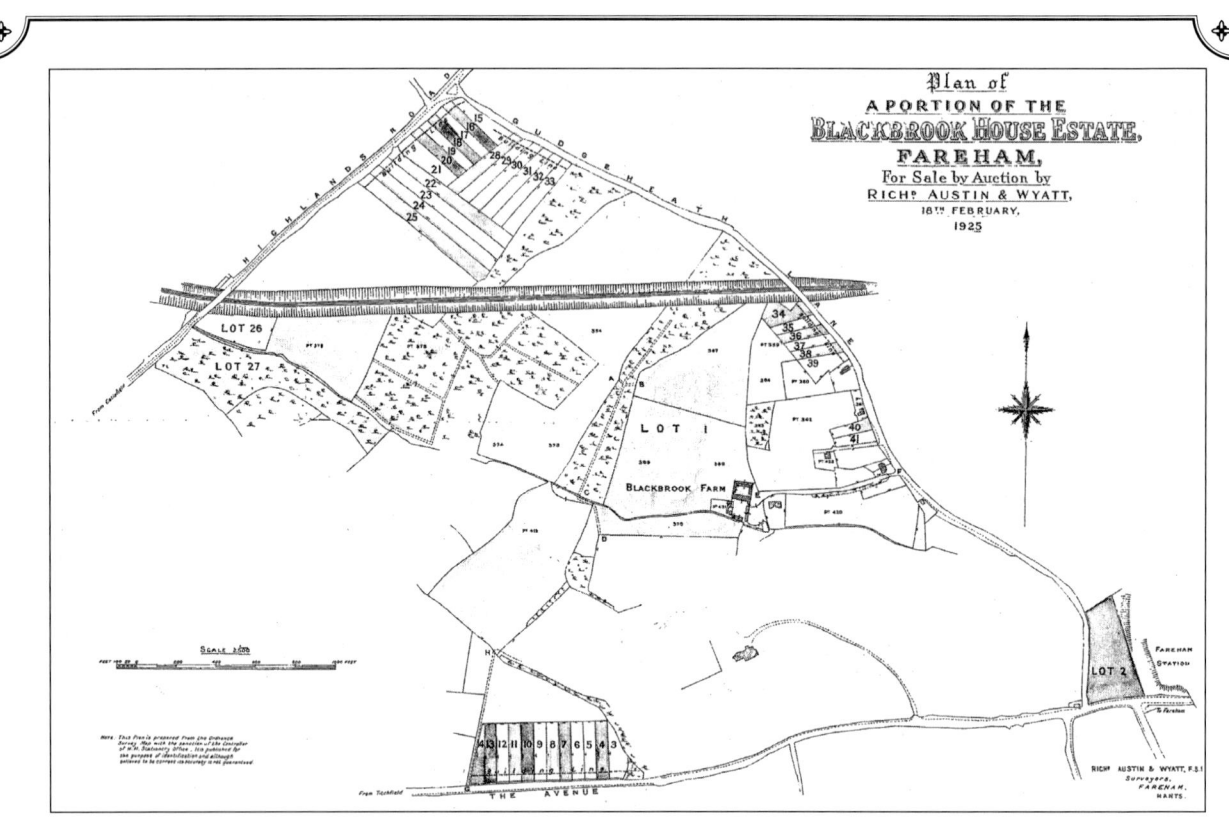

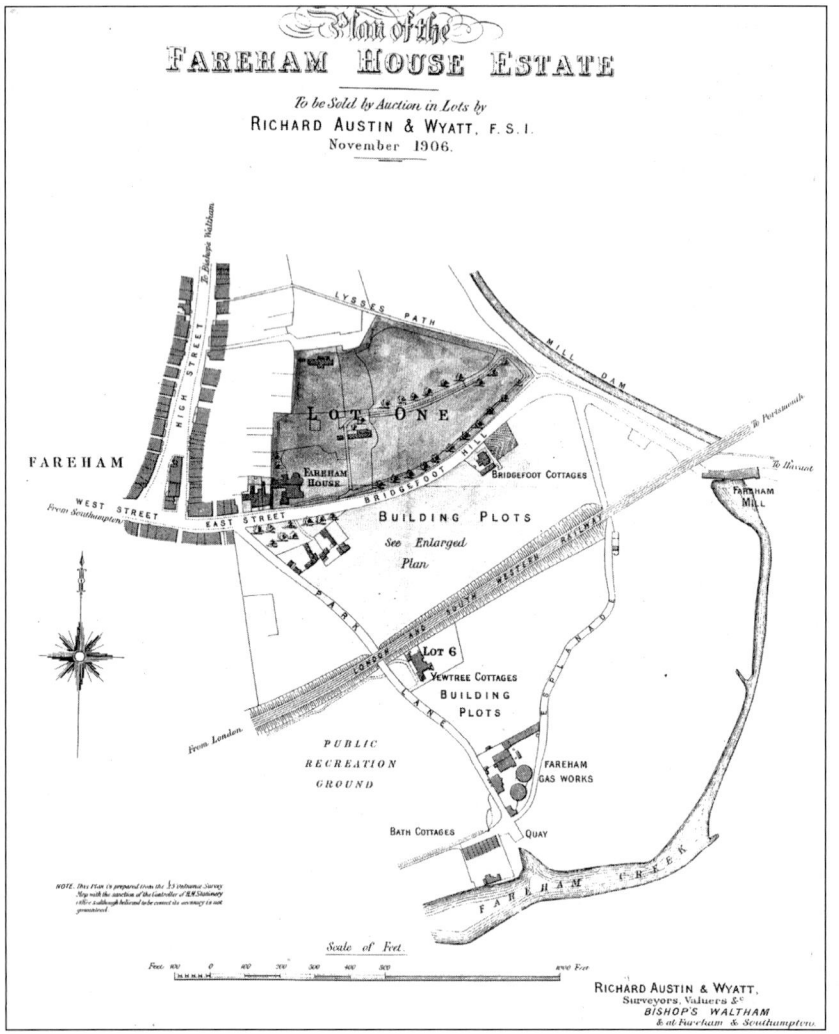

Above: *The plan of Blackbrook House estate, which was sold by auction in 1925.*

The plan of Fareham House estate and the surrounding area in 1906, when it was put up for auction.

THE BUILDINGS OF FAREHAM

Fareham House in East Street, in 2006 the premises of Wykeham House School. The rounded bays are echoed in some other High Street buildings, and by those at the rear of Cams Hall.

adapted for modern use, an indication that such old buildings can serve present needs without compromising Fareham's historic past.

One of Fareham's most attractive and distinctive buildings must be Blackbrook Cottage, renamed Bishopswood in 1927 when it became the official residence of the Bishops of Portsmouth. Built in the early-nineteenth century, it has a thatched roof and is in the style known as 'cottage orné'. The house has an intriguing connection with Jane Austen. Its original owner was Captain Thomas Maitland George Purvis, who was married to one of the novelist's nieces, Mary-Jane Austen, the eldest daughter of Admiral Francis Austen, himself no stranger to Fareham. The Purvises moved into Blackbrook Cottage after their marriage in 1828. There are some interesting stories recorded about the cottage, one of them being that a weeping willow by the pond was grown from a cutting taken from the grave of Napoleon Bonaparte on the island of St Helena. Another is that the cannonball finials on the entrance gate were brought back from Sebastopol by the eldest son of Mary-Jane and Captain Purvis, Herbert, who had served in the Crimean War.

At the time of its construction, Blackbrook Cottage was a subsidiary building to the more prestigious Blackbrook House. This handsome eighteenth-century house was the home for many years of the philanthropic Barton family. The original estate comprised more than 97 acres, with all the comforts and amenities a wealthy family of the period could desire: stables, parkland and extensive gardens. Blackbrook Cottage was acquired by the Portsmouth diocese after the estate was split up and sold by auctioneers Richard Austin & Wyatt for £14,000.

Fareham House, on the north side of East Street, is the home of Wykeham House School. Of late-eighteenth-century origin, the house was for many years the home of William Henry Deane, JP, who at the end of the nineteenth century moved from the now defunct Fairfield House on the south side of the street. Deane, a prominent figure in Fareham community life, owned all the land north of Fareham House and south down to the creek. He is best remembered today for his gift to the townspeople of the recreation ground at Bath Lane.

During the First World War, Fareham House became a military hospital. Dr W.S. Stevenson, who had served in the hospital, bought the house in 1919 and moved in with his wife, who had been a VAD Nurse in France during the war. The kitchen of Fareham House doubled as a consulting room and surgery. Five maids, a nanny and a governess supported the Stevenson family, the last-named lady still being alive in 1992 at the age of 94. Continuing its tradition of war service, Fareham House was the headquarters of the 35th Anti-Aircraft Brigade early in the Second World War. As such it was the opera-

The civic offices tower over Fareham town centre in this view from 2005. Opened officially in January 1977, the building is a familiar part of the local landscape and symbolises Fareham's modern outlook.

tional centre for the Portsmouth, Southampton and Isle of Wight anti-aircraft defences. After 1945 Fareham House had a variety of occupants, including the town's Social Security Department and Vospers, the shipbuilders.

As a monument to Fareham's famous brickmaking industry, the great viaduct across the creek still impresses and is a tribute to the skills and labour of the men who built it. Similarly, Forts Fareham, Wallington and Nelson are a reminder of Lord Palmerston's efforts to prevent French invasion. Fort Nelson is now a successful and popular military museum and events centre. Not so Forts Fareham and Wallington, both of which have become industrial estates. Thanks, however, to the 1901 census, we know something of the men who once served here. Fort Fareham housed the Royal Artillery, there being among the men a bombardier, four gunners and a cook, Adelaide Golding, and her nine-year-old son. Fort Wallington was the preserve of the Royal Grenadiers Artillery. There were five gunners, one Francis Butters with his wife and young daughter, and Acting Bombardier James Light, with his wife Liza and their five small children.

Of the great houses in Fareham, Rookesbury Park has always been associated with the Garnier family as Cams Hall has with the Delmes. Roche Court has connections with Peter des Roches, Bishop of Winchester in the early-thirteenth century, while Uplands was the home of Samuel Jellicoe, Henry Cort's associate. In the nineteenth century, Uplands was bought by John Beardmore. A renowned collector of arms and armour, Beardmore has had something of a renaissance in recent years since *Fareham Past and Present* serialised his very entertaining adolescent diaries.

Fareham today has several relatively new buildings which have successfully overcome prejudice from those quarters where anything modern is regarded with suspicion. The civic offices, formally opened in January 1977, at the time were regarded by some residents as a blot on the landscape, out of scale with their elegant neighbours in High Street. Since then, however, the building has blended into the life of the town, being visitor-friendly, spacious and rising over Fareham as a beacon for visitors and local people alike.

Dissent over the redevelopment of Cams Hall subsided once it became clear that the well-loved classical façade of the hall would be retained and restored to its original magnificence.

In Trinity Street, the Magistrates Courts had a mixed reception from the moment Hampshire County Council decided to build on this cramped site. The rather Moorish look of the architecture, it was thought, did not sit comfortably with the adjacent Victorian and Edwardian buildings. It was felt within the Fareham Society that the impact of a

The Magistrates' Courts in Trinity Street, December 2005.

building of this size and mass would have been lessened had there been room for a more gradual approaching vista to the entrance. Space, however, in all town centres, is at a premium and a luxury few local authorities can afford.

It is a fair prediction that in future years this building will join all the sites mentioned in this chapter to define the essence of Fareham's varied architectural heritage. Above all, it is the people who built these buildings and the people who lived in them who continue to fascinate all those interested in their local history.

Twenty-first century architecture. Part of the Market Quay development in the town centre in 2003. Strictly functional in style, Fareham's modern buildings are in sharp contrast to the elegant edifices in High Street, but it must be remembered that sound engineering principles always underlie such constructions. Although aesthetic criticisms are often to the detriment of modern buildings, the complicated planning and construction methods are rarely taken into account.

A 1979 view of No. 1, High Street, then Cook & Cook, the estate agents. For many years, earlier in the century, Montagu Warn carried on his millinery and drapery business in this building.

The same building in December 2005. It is now shared by estate agents Chapplins, and the High Street Newsagent. Note that the newsagent's window remains the same, while Chapplins have changed the frontage. Over the years, the upper part of No. 1 has been repainted in lighter colours, and the pedestrian guardrails are gone from the corner of the road.

❖ CHAPTER 15 ❖

Town in Transition

The first few years of the twentieth century saw few changes in the town. The tanning and brickmaking industries were perhaps beginning slowly to decline. At the quays, shipbuilding and marine businesses and industries still operated, albeit not quite so prominently as 50 years before. Once a week, Fareham's market provided plenty of bustling activity, but most of the time town life proceeded at a quiet, measured and reliable pace. The wealthy presided over the town from their homes in High Street or along the tree-lined roads to the west; the less well off inhabited small cottages in or around the town, often in the 'drokes' or little passageways off West Street. Most of the shops, comfortably providing all the necessities of life, were at the east end of West Street, while the west end, a section of which was dubbed 'Admirals Row' from the presumed occupation of its inhabitants, still mostly consisted of good houses.

A 1919 guide book drew attention to the pleasant situation of Fareham, mentioning the good blend of old and new houses and, in particular, the 'first-class shops'. Most of these were owned and operated by enterprising local inhabitants who knew how to cater for and adapt to the needs of the people. The perceived necessities of consumers at this time were simpler, perhaps, but Fareham's shopkeepers did not, on the whole, stint on display or service. Photographs of such shop frontages as that of J.H. Darby's hardware emporium at the corner of Quay Street, Egbert Neville's the chemists, Sutton's the stationers and Albion Dodge the drapers, for example, amply illustrate the pride which shopkeepers took in their premises. A sense of community imbued the town – one knew the local tradesmen, the doctors, the schoolteachers. Many tales are told of the little acts of kindness which epitomised Fareham life in the past, particularly in the economic decline of the 1930s, when many a tradesman or shopkeeper would arrange practical help for the more unfortunate local people by making sure they did not go hungry.

Changes were coming, however. During the 1930s Fareham's population grew rapidly, partly because of an increase in the demand for labour in the area's naval bases and also because the council absorbed extra communities, including Titchfield

A tram travelling along West Street on its way to Gosport from Fareham railway station, c.1910. On the right is the former Methodist Church and the small group of cottages including that in which Thackeray spent time in his childhood. Next to these are the Portland Buildings.

The western end of West Street, c.1930. Although there were still many private houses in the area at this time, such as those behind the trees to the right, shops were beginning to appear, including the millinery business of Sylvia Moss, seen here on the left.

and Portchester, into its administrative area. New housing estates appeared and, slowly but surely, motor traffic began to cause those problems of accessibility that have not been solved to this day. West Street, part of the main east–west A27 road, became polluted with the exhaust fumes of the ever-increasing traffic. By 1947 Fareham's population had risen to over 40,000, a 50 per cent increase in a mere 20 years. Town planners began to anticipate the difficulties Fareham would face if nothing was done. To this end Hampshire County Council and Portsmouth City Council combined with the local authority to commission a report on the perceived needs, prospects and future development of the area by the architect–planner Max Lock. He wrote:

The local development of work and social services has not kept pace with Fareham's growth of population. Local employment is on a small scale, and is mainly in the service industry. Social services such as libraries and community halls are few or are entirely lacking.

The shopping centre on West Street will need room for expansion and a new road system will help to divert traffic to the north of the town from its present path through the centre.

This report, produced in 1949, seems to have been the basis for the town's subsequent developments. The postwar race of growth was, indeed, quite astonishing in the area. Fareham's population increased even more than had been expected, with a particularly big rise of 38 per cent between 1961 and 1971. At the same time, in the congested streets of the town there were also changes in the shops. One by one the old family-owned businesses disappeared and were replaced by stores belonging to national chains. Photographs taken in the town in the 1950s show that the eastern end of West Street, in particular, was bustling with shoppers and traffic. West Street, fondly known as 'Golden Mile', was dubbed 'Nightmare Mile on the A27' by a local journalist.

In the frenetic pace that characterises the twenty-first century, there is a tendency for us to indulge in nostalgia. Many of us regard the Fareham of the mid-twentieth century as a timeless place, the very epitome of a comfortable market town, where everyone knew everyone else, where tastes were simpler, where nothing much changed. Although, inevitably, distance lends enchantment to the view, there was some truth behind these fond memories; certainly the shops provided those welcome touches of individuality and personal service that are perhaps absent today. Some of the shops had been trading for years, indeed for generations. One could hardly imagine Fareham without Dodge's the clothiers, Lusby's the grocers, Pyle's bakery, Batchelor's the chemists, Sutton's the stationers or Bizley's the confectioners and tobacconists, for example. During the 1950s and 1960s, new shops began to appear, particularly towards the western end of West Street, to cater for the needs of the rising population. Many former houses along from Trinity Church were converted into shops,

At the corner of Crescent Road, May 2005. Different services for the changing needs of society have taken over this area of West Street today. Businesses along the south side of the road include a supermarket and a car and motorcycle sales and accessories shop, while the former residences opposite have become offices of various kinds.

the wide pavements here being evidence of the former front gardens. Some piecemeal blocks of shops also appeared in this area, including the Co-operative Society's supermarket in 1958, the first in Fareham. This new type of shopping soon took hold, to the detriment of some former businesses, for example the first Tesco supermarket replaced Pyle's bakery in 1960 and the Victor Value supermarket was built on the corner of Westbury Road in 1961. This prominent new building later became another Tesco and, since 1983, has served the town as Argos.

Despite these changes, many of Fareham's newer inhabitants preferred to do their shopping in Portsmouth or Southampton, where there was more variety and choice of goods on offer. In addition, as the notion of tourism began to develop in the 1960s, there was evidence that visitors to the area tended to regard Fareham more as a place to stay while exploring other more interesting spots than as an attractive town in its own right. The council's solution to the fears that Fareham might stagnate in an economic sense was quite striking. In 1965, after much discussion, Shingler Risdon Associates was appointed to draw up a complete new plan for the town centre and surrounds, thereby confirming the council's intention to take firm control of Fareham's destiny rather than adopt the laissez-faire attitude to growth of many other towns and cities.

The architects concluded that Fareham did not offer the variety of retail choice that its large population required, criticising the previous unplanned development of the shopping centre and remarking that 'this ribbon-type commercial development has produced an uneconomic sterilisation of valuable backland.' A new town-centre map was produced, with the suggestion that development should take place between Quay Street and the north of West Street. Within this area, a large shopping precinct, linked to car parks and new civic buildings, it was suggested, should be provided to stimulate Fareham's potential as a vibrant and important economic centre. Also recommended was the provision of extra shopping facilities south of West Street between Hartlands Road and Quay Street, together with two dual carriageways running north and south of the A27 to enable through traffic to by-pass the town centre and link with the proposed new motorway. Other suggestions included the building of maisonettes and flats, a new library and new civic hall, an art gallery and museum, and also a community

Here is Western Road in the mid 1950s, a quiet cul-de-sac not far from the Methodist church. Today this scene is much changed as many of the houses have been demolished and the noisy and busy Western Way runs alongside.

New Road, which leads off Gordon Road and branches right to face the rear of houses in Colenso Road, pictured here in the 1950s. A former Fareham resident who had lived in Canada for over 50 years returned on a family visit in 1985 and found Gordon Road and the surrounding streets little changed since his boyhood, except for the parked vehicles in every bit of available space outside the houses!

TOWN IN TRANSITION

A Tom Parker Dairies van is the only motor vehicle to be seen in this 1950s view of Deane's Park Road near Bath Lane and the creek. The road is named after the former owner of Fareham House, William Deane, who owned land in this area and made a gift of the recreation ground to the people of Fareham.

centre overlooking the shopping precinct.

Such a plan was not just a facelift, it was totally revolutionary. Many local people welcomed it; others feared it would result in the wholesale destruction of their town. Some said it would never happen. But, of course, with many modifications, it did. The council agreed that, in principle, the plans were to be adopted. In 1971 the new scheme was presented to the county council, which gave outline permission for the first phase to begin.

By this time, parts of the proposed road recommendations had already been implemented. The eastern half of the southern town bypass, begun in 1968, ran parallel to the railway line and met Portchester Road at a new roundabout. During the same year, the far west end of the town underwent a major change when the old arched railway bridge was replaced by a less attractive but more functional construction. At the same time, the approach road from the town was widened, resulting in the demolition of the Cremer cottages and the West End inn. The old railway bridge had been a bottleneck for years, double-decker buses and large lorries having to move into the centre of the road in order to clear the arches. The new double bridge provided uniform height above a wider road. A long-term resident recalls the old bridge:

I remember often having to wait for ages to go under the bridge – for some reason, the chequered decoration on the brickwork and in particular the big 'Brockhouse' advertisement across the top seem indelibly printed on my mind!

The improvements certainly temporarily alleviated some of the traffic jams, but the vast increase in traffic since then still leaves drivers, at peak times, stuck in two lanes of traffic around this spot.

Greater changes in the roads were soon to follow. As the first part of the M27 South Coast motorway was constructed in 1972, in Fareham work began on the western link road running from the A27 via a roundabout near the railway station to connect with the eastern bypass by way of another roundabout. During the same year the council approved a £1,136,000 scheme in the hope of alleviating another notorious blackspot, Gosport Road between Town Quay and Newgate Lane. This involved widening the road, which meant the demolition of some houses, a petrol station and the Baptist Church, and the building of pedestrian bridges. The new schemes caused controversy. A.H. Barrett, chairman of Fareham Residents' Association, pointed out that the council had already admitted that another new road would eventually have to be built across the creek to cope with future traffic; therefore, he argued, it would make more sense to consider this idea first, thus saving time, money and the considerable costs of compensation and rehabilitation arising from the demolition of existing buildings. Eventually,

THE BOOK OF FAREHAM

Union Street, once home to Fareham Union Workhouse, looking towards High Street, c.1956. This little road, with its mixture of fascinating old buildings, sometimes goes unnoticed by visitors admiring the adjacent High Street.

TOWN IN TRANSITION

The same view along Union Street 50 years later, in December 2005. Apart from cosmetic changes and the removal of chimneys, this mysterious corner of old Fareham remains largely unchanged.

Union Street looking towards East Street, December 2005. In the distance, the corner of the Red Lion Hotel can be seen; the three-storey building to its left, formerly a warehouse, is built of Fareham Reds.

The eastern end of West Street c.1910. The first three shops on the left are businesses that served the people of Fareham for many years: Sutton's the stationer, Batchelor's the chemist and Dunn's the gentlemen's outfitter.

By the end of the 1950s the eastern end of West Street had become very busy with vehicles and shoppers. On the left is Pyle's bakery with its RAC-recommended restaurant, a popular spot which exuded lovely aromas of fresh baking. A few years later this became the site for one of Fareham's first supermarkets, Tesco. Next door is Dodge's the clothiers, while the first four-storey building a few doors along is Batchelor's the chemist. The interesting line of cars inching towards High Street corner includes a Standard 8 and an Austin A35.

TOWN IN TRANSITION

The busy town centre on a wet December day in the 1950s. The trees atop the lighting standards are a striking and unusual decorative motif for the Christmas season. The bus station is on the left, while the World's Stores, Bata shoe shop and the Savoy cinema can be seen on the right.

A bus passes the Embassy cinema and Tesco's – in 2006 the Argos store – in the late 1970s. Tesco once had two sites in Fareham, the smaller, of which was built at the corner of Church Path, replacing Pyle's bakery. At the time of writing the giant supermarket chain is hoping to gain permission to build a large new superstore on the site of the old forge in Quay Street.

The driver of the Standard car signals with his arm that he is about to turn right into Wallington Hill, c.1955. The Provincial bus is travelling up High Street between Lysses House and the Golden Lion, while the Morris is passing the end of Osborn Road.

Basketware and plants on sale at the lower corner of the market in the 1970s. Hartlands Road can be seen in the background. Part of this area has since become the bus station and the FirstBus travel shop.

TOWN IN TRANSITION

The crane in the background indicates that the first phase of Fareham's new shopping precinct is under way behind the soon-to-be-transformed face of West Street in 1972.

The construction of the Station Roundabout and the Western Way relief road necessitated a high-level pedestrian overpass, from which this 1970s view of the station forecourt and railway bridge was taken. Cockerills factory (to the right) became the Crown Bingo building and later the Prague Junction night club.

Major roadworks took place in 1986 in an attempt to ease the congestion in and out of Fareham on the Gosport and Lee roads. This photograph, taken in August 1986, shows work on the overpass which leads to Newgate Lane. Despite these changes, which included the widening of Gosport Road into a dual carriageway at the approach to the viaduct, the roads hereabouts are often gridlocked during the rush hour.

however, the road-widening went ahead, despite further complaints from those elderly and infirm residents forced to use the overbridges to reach the town from certain streets; a pelican crossing was later installed across Gosport Road.

Despite the costs and the genuine efforts of planners, in 2006 the traffic problems along the approach roads to Fareham are still severe. The Quay Roundabout, at present, is not a comfortable prospect for the faint-hearted driver, particularly when travelling from the town towards Gosport or Lee-on-the-Solent. And as for the oft-proposed road bridge across the creek – will it remain, like the name of a pleasant and popular nearby pub, a 'castle in the air'?

✤ CHAPTER 16 ✤

To the Millennium and Beyond

A view over the town westwards from the roof of the civic offices in June 1979. The north entrance to the shopping precinct is to the left, with the library in the foreground and the multi-storey car park behind. The raised area to the right with parked cars and clumps of trees was soon to be the site of the Ferneham Hall. Holy Trinity Church spire can be seen top left, just along from the flat front of Foresters' Hall, while Osborn Road stretches away on the right towards Gordon Road in the distance.

During the 1970s the old market town character that had once epitomised Fareham disappeared forever. What emerged to take its place, while a delight to some, was anathema to others. In 1972 the huge redevelopment scheme, comprising a shopping precinct with 140,000sq.ft of retail space, civic buildings including the local authority health centre, a large multi-storey car park and a new library, was begun. Soon there was building work everywhere in the east end of the town.

The impact that the new scheme to transform Fareham might have was not lost on local people. Many comments appeared in the press, ranging from the sensible to the ridiculous. Some praised the foresight shown by the Borough Council in realising that a future Fareham would need shopping and social facilities far above and beyond the existing ones. Phrases such as 'giving the town centre a new heart', 'a development way above the standard of centres in the south's two main cities' and 'making sure the growing population in the borough will do their shopping in Fareham' appeared in the press. Local retailers had mixed reactions to the new shopping centre. Some were in favour, arguing that the new development would provide vitality to Fareham's economic life; but others, particularly those whose shops were situated at the west end of West Street, feared that their trade would be taken away as a result of the new shops at the other end of the town. The multi-storey car park came in for criticism on

139

Fareham's new look in June 1979. The West Street frontage of the shopping precinct, with the children's play area to the right, provides a striking contrast to earlier scenes of busy traffic and older shopfronts.

By September 2005 the scene is somewhat less pristine and stark, with the introduction of a few trees, newly styled porches and the millennium sculptures and paving in place.

both aesthetic and efficacy grounds – 'no one will use it!' came the cry, especially when the council decided to charge 5p. for its use.

By the mid-1970s the first phase of the new town centre development was complete. The huge civic office complex towered above the town, symbolising change and modernity. Many found the new shopping precinct, with its air-conditioned environment, seats and, of course, new shops, quite unusual. 'It's strange,' observed one woman shopper, 'when you are in the precinct, it doesn't seem as though you are in Fareham any more.' Another was delighted: 'It's much bigger than I expected inside. And there's much more choice.' A writer in the *Southern Evening Echo* in June 1976 found the combination of old and new Fareham very pleasing:

It seems impossible, looking at the present-day crowds

✤ TO THE MILLENNIUM AND BEYOND ✤

Inside the shopping mall, June 1979, looking towards Westbury Square. Both Gamley's toy shop (on the left) and Martin's newsagents (on the right) – are long since gone.

A shopper walks towards the lifts of the multi-storey car park, June 1979.

milling around the large shops to believe that it was ever the quiet, dull little town that any of us remember... the new Thackeray Mall shopping precinct has a garden-like restaurant which almost persuades one that its green and white tables are laid in the open air.

As well as the cafe-restaurant – in 2006 Giardino's – the precinct had over 60 shops and even a public house, long-since gone, where, at the time of writing, Ottakar's bookshop stands. Once the novelty had worn off, more dissenting voices began to be heard. Some said the shops were not interesting enough, and one critic claimed that before long Fareham would become a ghost town. Nevertheless, the first Christmas in the new precinct saw some pretty substantial ghosts! And despite the uncertain economic climate of the late 1970s the new precinct and the town centre in general continued to thrive.

The Garden Restaurant in the shopping mall, June 1979, with Sainsbury's supermarket in the background.

In 2006 Café Giardino occupies the area of the earlier Garden Restaurant, as seen here in December 2001. Sainsbury's moved from the precinct in the 1990s and relocated to Broadcut.

141

Town centre redevelopment undertaken from the 1970s did not only affect West Street. Portland Street, seen here looking towards Woolworth's in the early 1980s, was a busy thoroughfare until the changes resulted in the demolition of houses, shops and pubs, and when the Market Quay scheme came to fruition the street ceased to exist. Hansford's fishing tackle shop, Ken's the barber's and the fish and chip shop seen here are but a distant memory.

One letter in the local press praised the new facilities in glowing terms, enthusing about the:

... cool, clean, attractive and delightful atmosphere... my grateful thanks to Fareham planners for providing such a service which is in such obvious contrast with that provided by Portsmouth in Commercial Road, the Tricorn and North End.

By the end of 1976, the success of the precinct, now named Westbury Mall, was assured. The arrival of a large branch of Marks & Spencer not only brought in more shoppers but also created a further 130 new jobs. As a local woman remarked:

For the first time ever, I can do all my Christmas shopping here in the town, and I don't have to go to the cities with all that travel and crowds.

A visitor from Southampton, writing in the local press, thought that Fareham had the best of both worlds, and praised the new mall for its 'up and coming look' whilst still finding much to enjoy in visiting the older shops, many of which, as she pointed out, still bore names known in the town for many generations and which still took a pride in providing personal services to their customers.

This balance between old and new was a precarious one, however. One by one, the long-established

The boarded-up houses at the southern end of Portland Street await their demise in the march of progress.

names on the shopfronts began to disappear as the shiny new precinct's undoubted attractions and advantages began to draw trade away. In 1981 the precinct was enlarged; at the same time once-familiar Fareham shops including Phillips's, Sutton's, Dodge's, Vimpany's and Burt's closed down. There was opposition from some quarters to these changes. The Fareham Society urged the council to reappraise the ongoing town centre plan in the hope that further development would not merely entail the provision of yet more shops. A pressure group produced a number of articles under the banner 'Shop Fresh Air Fareham', which encouraged people to make more

✣ TO THE MILLENNIUM AND BEYOND ✣

When Beagley's wool shop in West Street was demolished in 1985, the structure was discovered to be of Tudor or even earlier origins. Here the ancient framework is exposed to the elements for the first time in centuries.

By 1983 the days of busy traffic polluting this part of West Street were long gone. Here the former fire station, the Woolwich premises, the United Reformed Church and the Portland Buildings bask in the sunshine near an attractive area of greenery. In 2006 only the former church and Portland Buildings survive; the Woolwich, which relocated to a unit in the new Market Quay scheme, was the first business to open for business in the new development.

A closer view of the timber construction of the building.

use of the remaining local shops outside the precinct. Concerns were also raised that the new chainstores, however convenient for shoppers, were not providing the same service to the local community as had their predecessors.

By the 1990s, all of those once revolutionary and talked-about new buildings – the civic offices, the library, the car park and the shopping precinct itself – had become familiar and commonplace parts of Fareham. Indeed, by 1998, the indoor precinct, then called the Fareham Shopping Centre, was beginning to show its age. A whole new generation of shopping centres, including the nearby Gunwharf in Portsmouth and West Quay in Southampton, had arisen by then, in comparison with which that at Fareham suddenly seemed old-fashioned and dull. In response to declining patronage, Fareham Shopping Centre was given a £15 million makeover which included the installation of glass roofing to provide a lighter, fresher feeling to the interior and the replacement of all walls and floors, together with new entrances, new toilets, new cafés and larger shopfronts. Television personality Fern Britton proved a popular choice to perform the official re-launching of the centre in November 1998.

The facelift of Fareham centre was the first part of another new phase in the town's life involving further major rebuilding works, as Fareham moved into the twenty-first century with plans for the regeneration of West Street and the development of Market Quay. The West Street scheme was the Henry Cort Millennium Project. This imaginative idea involved the provision of a permanent street exhibition, in the year 2000, to celebrate the work of the ironmaster Henry Cort, who had developed his revolutionary processes in Fontley and Gosport in the 1780s. The project, which was awarded a grant of £641,000 by the Millennium Commission, took the form of a collection of sculptural ironworks produced by world-renowned artist–blacksmiths. Local shoppers looked on with fascination as the various sculptures were erected along the pedestrian arm of West Street. Each of the pieces has some symbolic significance –the Performance Podium, designed by Kate Maddison, for instance, was intended to suggest both the nautical and market traditions of Fareham, while the three figures made by Ryszard Mazur were based

Despite all the upheaval in the town centre, some older buildings remain along the north side of West Street, as seen here in May 2005. The smaller building in the centre was once Milbank's the butchers, the Sony shop was Phillips's ladies' wear, and the Daily Echo *premises once housed the long-established stationers and booksellers, Sutton's.*

on photographs taken of shoppers in the precinct. Michael Haase's commemorative plaque features pictures of Cort's furnace, forge hammer and grooved rollers, outlined in wrought iron. All of the sculptures, incorporating the use of wrought iron, were made using techniques typical of those available in Cort's lifetime. In addition to the sculptures, a children's play area was designed by Andy Frost with the active support at the drawing stage of pupils from Ranvilles Junior School.

Part of the Monday market in West Street, July 2004. The Framing Centre formerly housed the Home & Colonial Stores, while the British Heart Foundation charity shop was once Faye's fashion shop; however, Bateman's the opticians, have traded from their building for many years.

TO THE MILLENNIUM AND BEYOND

A clothing stall at the Monday market in July 2004, near the Crown pub in West Street. The Crown, which was the inn nearest to the former market site, no doubt in the past provided much relief for farmers after a hard day's trading.

Locks Heath became a major area of redevelopment in the borough during the 1970s and 1980s. Besides new housing, a large shopping centre, a library, a health centre, a community centre and a Police Station were all built under the aegis of a scheme known as Locks Heath Centre and Park. Here, in July 1983, construction is well under way. The large building on the right became the Co-op superstore.

The former Magistrates' Courts in Trinity Street shortly before demolition.

The controversial styling of the new Magistrates' Courts, built in 1994, seen here on a damp December day in 2005.

Work in West Street proceeding towards the completion of the Henry Cort Millennium Project, February 2000. The Performance Podium can be seen in the centre, while the new street lamps display banners announcing the arrival of the permanent exhibition, which was formally opened in April 2000.

Five years into the new millennium, the wrought iron sculptures and street furniture, familiar features of the town, include 'The Smith Tree Of Life' near the corner of Quay Street. Day's Buildbase store, on the right, in 2006 has become the Cafe Tusk Indian restaurant.

The sculpture entitled 'The Horn Of Plenty', the stones tumbling from the iron basket representing fruit from the market.

View from the edge of the car park of Woolworth's and the Savoy Buildings, January 2002. Work was soon to begin on the shops which now line this side of the street.

The framework of the new shops rises during the spring of 2003. Behind the building work can be seen the museum, while one of the millennium sculptures is on the right.

The building work further advanced, July 2003.

An interested observer near the flower stall reads about the Market Quay development outside what, in May 2004, would become TKMaxx.

One of the 'shoppers' sculptures outside the new Robert Dyas store in January 2005.

TO THE MILLENNIUM AND BEYOND

In the summer of 2005 work proceeds on the conversion of the former United Reformed Church. The chain just seen on the far left is part of the 'Still Moves' sculpture.

Spring shoppers in West Street, May 2005.

The Savoy Buildings viewed from the front of the museum, May 2005.

Sainsbury's supermarket, seen here in November 2005. On the wall of the supermarket is an interesting plaque by David Backhouse which depicts children through the ages against a backdrop of Fareham landmarks.

147

In the first week of January 2006 the converted church provides the background to the Performance Podium, still twinkling with Christmas lights.

The elegant wrought-iron gateway commemorating the Queen's golden jubilee of 2002, photographed in January 2006. When it was moved from its original site nearer the precinct to a position between the Quay roundabout and the Market Quay car park, some controversy arose concerning the fact that not many people walked along this part of the road. At the time of writing, however, the council plans to construct a tree-lined walkway from the gate through the car park to the Market Quay shops.

The new streetscape was enhanced by specially designed new light standards with brackets to hold banners and supports for large flower baskets. New paving areas featured materials designed to provide an appropriate balance to the sculptures. In 2006 the various items of the Henry Cort project are a familiar part of the West Street scene. As with all projects of this type, there has been much local discussion as to the lasting impression. There have been criticisms that the various pieces are too scattered and that they might have been built closer together in order to focus attention on them. Some feel that the shop buildings erected since have tended to dominate the sculptures somewhat, while others believe the works to be too abstract. Many local people, however, are delighted that Fareham has gained a unique, idiosyncratic and permanent exhibition which reflects part of the town's history. Many children, in particular, enjoy Stephen Lunn's Anvil Man, a light-hearted sculpture sponsored by the Old Priceans which stands near where William Price started his original school.

Since the millennium, the third and final phase of Fareham's town-centre revitalisation programme has proceeded apace. During the changes some familiar buildings have been demolished, some preserved and one in particular, the former United Reformed Church of 1836, transformed. This Grade II listed edifice has been refurbished and a glass extension added in which the tall windows echo the Gothic style of the original church. It is destined to become a bar-restaurant, a future which devout worshippers at the original church would have found incomprehensible, but which somehow rather ruefully reflects life in twenty-first-century Britain!

In July 2005 the Borough Council marked the official opening of the Market Quay scheme with a special day of events entitled 'Fareham Celebrates'. The new complex contains facilities in keeping with the fast pace of modern life, including a fitness centre, two cafés and a sandwich bar, besides several nationally known retail stores and the five-screen Apollo Cinema. It is a pity that some of the original proposals, such as those for a tower and for decorative features on the surrounding walls, were omitted from the final scheme on the grounds of cost. One pleasing outcome, however is the naming of two of the routes within the Market Quay: Cremer Mall, named after the town's former benefactor and Nobel Prize winner, and Harper Way, named in memory of Malcolm Harper, Fareham's first honorary alderman and a councillor for 15 years, who worked tirelessly to help so many community groups in the town.

Thus Fareham has changed from the market town of a century ago into the busy centre it is today, epitomised by the bustle of Market Quay. What will happen in the future no-one can predict, but, as the legend on the Borough crest assures us, Fareham will always be *Prest A Faire* – 'Ready To Do'.

CHAPTER 17

Some Fareham Personalities

Edward Lyon Berthon (1813–1899)

Edward Berthon was born in 1813 in London. He trained to become a doctor but abandoned the idea of a career in medicine and entered the church instead. Always fascinated by boats and mechanics, he possessed practical as well as imaginative skills and invented a two-bladed screw propeller during the 1830s. When he demonstrated his prototype to the Admiralty, the board declared the idea unworkable. Undeterred, he produced what has come to be known as 'Berthon's Log', a device to measure the suction pressures produced on a boat passing through water.

After he was ordained, Berthon served as a curate for a short time in Lymington and in 1845 was appointed to Holy Trinity Church in Fareham. Besides bringing a zealous approach to pastoral affairs in his new parish, he carried on with his marine experiments, developing the log further and also working on the manufacture of calibration gauges to measure the trim and rolling of boats at sea. In 1849 he designed and built his most enduring invention, a collapsible boat designed for easy transportation on expeditions and in warfare. It is reported that Revd Berthon actually tested a version of this boat in the cellar beneath the church, which had become flooded after a particularly heavy storm!

Holy Trinity Church, January 2006.

The new boat was demonstrated at Netley before Queen Victoria – but again the Admiralty board were not keen on the innovative new vessel. In 1860 Berthon left Holy Trinity and took up the living at Romsey Abbey, where he carried on his experiments. His folding boats became a success, Sir George Nares taking them on his expedition to the Arctic, while General Gordon had them sent to him at Khartoum.

Berthon died in 1899. His memorial in Romsey Abbey, where he also undertook an energetic programme of renovation and improvements, is a fine window which shows both the inventor and his collapsible boat.

Henry Cort (1740–1800)

Henry Cort was the son of a brickmaker and builder. His wife, Elizabeth Heysham, was the niece of a certain Mr Attwick, who supplied the naval dockyards with various iron chains and other stores. Attwick sold his contract to a Gosport man, Thomas Morgan, in 1772, and Henry Cort took over Morgan's Gosport premises at The Green in 1775. Besides supplying the dockyard with iron materials, Cort also began to experiment with the processes of manufacturing iron. In 1779 he took over a large forge at Fontley in order to test out his new methods of iron puddling. It is thought that at least one other forge was in use in this area just north of Fareham; there was plenty of timber for fuelling a forge, and the River Meon supplied the water-power necessary to work the tilt hammers.

Cort found a backer for his expensive experiments in Adam Jellicoe, a naval paymaster who invested £27,500 in the Fareham enterprise. At first all went well. Cort's genius and the single-mindedness he applied to his experiments produced great improvements in the quality of manufactured iron, as well as in the speed with which it could be produced. He patented his methods and, after detailed study, the Navy pronounced Cort's processes a great success. After 1787 they decided to use his type of iron to cast anchors and chains for naval vessels instead of the Swedish and Russian iron they had previously bought, while other ironmasters in Britain paid royalties to Cort to use his processes. By 1789 the British iron industry was producing 68,000 tons of iron a year – before Cort had come on the scene, the figure was only 17,000 tons a year. Cort carried out further improvements at Fontley, while his Gosport forge produced the orders.

In 1789, however, through no fault of his own, Cort's enterprise was cruelly compromised when it was discovered that his backer, Adam Jellicoe, had 'borrowed' the money he had invested in the business from the Navy Pay Office. The day after he was asked to explain this misappropriation of funds, Jellicoe was found dead, a possible suicide. As Cort had pledged his patents to Jellicoe as security, besides giving over half his stock and profits, he was now held responsible for the debts. Quickly his patents were seized and his outstanding contracts given to other ironmasters, who in turn ruthlessly broke their agreements to pay royalties to Cort.

The great ironmaster was ruined and forced into bankruptcy. His businesses at Gosport and Fontley were taken over, ironically, by Samuel Jellicoe, son of his former partner. Cort and his large family moved to London, where he lived out the last years of his life in poverty mitigated by a pension from the government and a paltry collection on his behalf arranged by some of the same ironmasters who had profited from his downfall. He died in 1860, as his tombstone in Hampstead cemetery pathetically remarks, 'a broken man'. The Fontley forge and mill continued working until the 1850s, though on a much-reduced scale. This comment on the sad decline of the works was written in 1852:

Two old men, each probably over 80 years of age, were the solitary workmen... the following year the two ancient craftsmen either ceased their labours or went over to the majority and Funtley (sic) *was now no longer known as a foundry.*

Today Cort's memory is perpetuated in the Henry Cort School, in a road, Cort Way and, above all, in the Henry Cort millennium sculptures. These permanent exhibits along West Street, made using only the techniques and materials contemporary with the ironmaster's time, are a fitting tribute to one of Fareham's great sons.

Sir William Randal Cremer (1828–1908)

William Randal Cremer was born in Fareham in 1828, the son of a coach-painter. Already poor, the family's condition worsened when his father deserted them while William was only a child. In 1843 William was apprenticed to his uncle, a builder, and became a carpenter and joiner. He became very interested in the burgeoning initiatives to improve the lot of the working man and, on moving to London in 1852, became active in the trade union movement. He organised support for the reduction of the working day to nine hours and founded the Amalgamated Society of Carpenters and Joiners in 1860. Convinced that peace was the natural mode of existence for all the peoples in the world, Cremer strongly supported the idea of international arbitration rather than war to settle potential conflicts.

In 1870 he organised a group of working men to advocate England's neutrality at the time of the Franco-Prussian War, a movement which led to the foundation of the Workmen's Peace Association in 1871. The new organisation was very successful and led in turn to establishment of the International Arbitration League. In 1885 this tireless worker for peace and the poor also became a vigorous Member of Parliament for Haggerston in London's poverty-stricken East End. In 1903, as a result of his tireless work, he was awarded the Nobel Peace Prize, which included a stipend of £8,000, a huge sum in those days. Typically, Cremer gave nearly all of the money to the International Arbitration League, even though he was in relatively straitened circumstances himself. His selfless efforts were rewarded with a knighthood in 1907, the year before his death.

Not forgetting the town of his birth, Cremer set up

Henry Cort, ironmaster. A powerful portrait of the man whose development of the wrought-iron process speeded up production and helped satisfy the massive demand for iron in the nineteenth century.

SOME FAREHAM PERSONALITIES

Fareham Society's plaque for Randal Cremer is put into position on 1 October 1994. Left to Right: Brenda Clapperton (Secretary), Ron Short (Chairman), Sir Ian Lloyd MP, Sir Richard Marshall MP (President of the Inter-Parliamentary Union) and Roy Perry MEP.

Cremer's birthplace, No. 124 West Street, is commemorated by this blue plaque provided by the Fareham Society. His former house is now part of a shop.

By January 2006, though the shops have different names, the plaque remains in honour of Fareham's Nobel Peace Prize winner.

The sign 'Cremer Mall' on the corner wall of the Subway sandwich shop. Note also the sign 'Pulheim Parade' on the right, evidencing Fareham's link with its twin town in Germany.

the group of Cremer cottages at the far western end of West Street, which sadly were demolished at the time of the road-widening and rebuilding of the railway bridge. New cottages bearing his name, however, were erected later in Stubbington. Happily, today he is acknowledged through the Randal Cremer Trust, a charitable body whose aim is to continue to provide almshouses for the poor or severely disabled. In Fareham, his name has been given to one of the new walkways within Market Quay – Cremer Mall.

151

Sir John Goss (1800–1880)

Goss, born in Fareham, showed early promise in music. His fine treble voice gained him a place as a Chapel Royal chorister in 1811 and by the time he was in his twenties he was composing sacred music, including hymns and anthems, his best-loved hymn being 'Praise My Soul the King of Heaven'. He was appointed an instructor at the Royal Academy of Music, where his favourite pupil was Arthur Sullivan, the musical half of the world-famous comic opera duo. In 1876, both master and pupil received their Doctorates of Music at the same ceremony. Goss was devoted to Sullivan but urged him to concentrate on more serious music: 'I hope you may become a worthy composer and the greatest of symphonists,' he wrote.

Goss enjoyed the gratitude of Queen Victoria when, in 1871, he composed a *Te Deum* for the public thanksgiving for the recovery from serious illness of the Prince of Wales. The work was performed in St Paul's Cathedral, where Goss had been appointed organist in 1838. A commemorative plaque records his birthplace in High Street.

Arthur Hamilton Lee (1868–1947)

Arthur Lee was the Member of Parliament for South Hampshire, the constituency of which Fareham was a part between 1900 and 1922. He was born in Bridport in 1868, the son of Melville Lee, rector of St Mary's, Bridport and Emily Dicker. His father died when Arthur was only a child, and his mother, left with little money, placed him in the care of others. He was sent to various boarding schools, eventually becoming an Army officer and then, thanks to his appetite for hard work and administrative skills, serving as a diplomat in Canada and the United States. Later, his mother came to live in Fareham at No. 12 High Street.

In 1899 Lee married the daughter of a wealthy American banker and returned to England to seek a career in politics. In 1900 he was adopted as the Conservative candidate for South Hampshire at the time of the General Election, meeting the constituency association at Fareham in June. He described his opponent as 'an honest but unimpressive little man with the unfortunate name of Tweedy-Smith' and adopted the use of a horse-drawn coach-and-four to tour the area, believing that his Liberal rival would harm his own chances by driving around Fareham 'in a chugging and evil-smelling car'. Lee certainly made his mark – he doubled the existing Conservative majority.

As the local Member of Parliament, Lee, together with his wife, was soon busy not only with

Sir John Goss, Fareham's most famous musician.

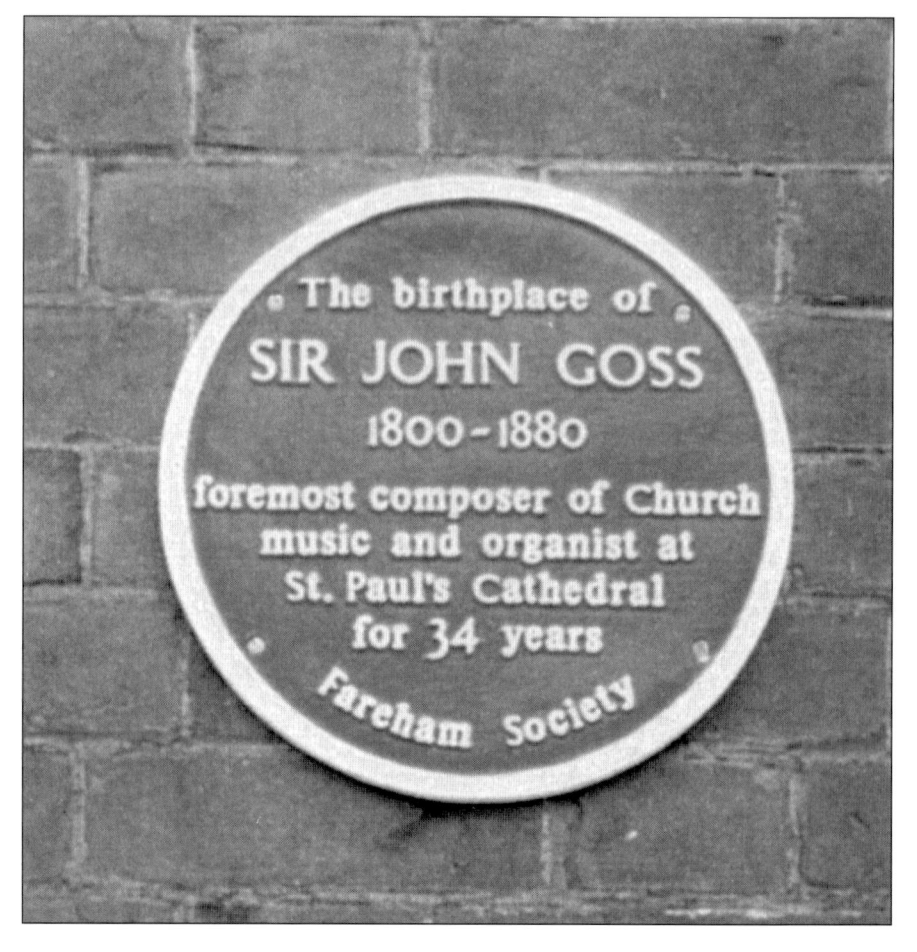

Goss was born at No. 21 High Street, where the Fareham Society placed this plaque in memory of this great composer of church music.

SOME FAREHAM PERSONALITIES

Long-serving local Member of Parliament Viscount Lee of Fareham is rather amusingly recalled in his constituency town by this modern pub, the Lord Arthur Lee! This picture of the pub in West Street was taken in January 2006.

constituency work but also in the social milieu. The couple rented the Georgian house Rookesbury Park at Wickham, where they entertained the leading lights of Fareham society. Lee bought a new 12h.p. Lanchester car – presumably one less offensive than that of his opponent at the 1900 General Election!

During the First World War Lee was appointed Military Secretary to the coalition government Prime Minister, Lloyd George, later becoming Director-General of Food Production and, for a short period after the war, First Lord of the Admiralty. At this time Lee owned the large country house known as Chequers, which he generously donated to the country for the permanent use of prime ministers. In 1922 he was elevated to the House of Lords as Viscount Lee of Fareham. Thereafter, however, his political ambitions were thwarted – it is said he was too ambitious, too intolerant, and was not popular with many influential members of the Conservative Party. Viscount Lee turned to other interests later in life; he was a collector of paintings and fine art and was a founder, with Samuel Courtauld, of the Courtauld Institute of Art. A generous man, he presented a valuable collection of gold, silver and bronze pieces, dating from the Renaissance, to the people of Canada in recognition of their efforts during the Second World War. This impressive collection is housed in the Royal Ontario Museum.

Lee died in 1947. His name is recalled today not by a street, road or statue, but by a pub – the Lord Arthur Lee, one of Fareham's newer hostelries along West Street. This memorial might well have tickled the Viscount's quirky sense of humour.

William Makepeace Thackeray (1811–1863)

Born in Calcutta, India, Thackeray was the only child of Richard Makepeace Thackeray and his wife Anne. Thackeray senior was in India as Collector, then Secretary to the Calcutta Board of Revenue. This is a period in English history when upwardly mobile young men from good families went east to make, hopefully, a name and a lucrative career for themselves with the East India Company.

Young Thackeray did not have a happy childhood. His father died when William was three years old. Shortly afterwards his mother sent him home to England with an even younger cousin. At first the two boys went to stay with their Aunt Ritchie in

The house with the bay windows was where the novelist Thackeray spent much of his childhood. This row of old houses was demolished in the 1930s to make way for the bus station. In the early years of the twentieth century, Fareham's first library was established in Thackeray's house.

London. Here they went to school at Walpole House, then later to a boarding school at the Polygon, Southampton. The youthful William detested school, the most enjoyable part of his time at Southampton being when he was taken to the theatre. His near contemporary, Charles Dickens, had a similarly bad childhood and also loved the theatre. Both authors initially pursued careers in journalism and law. Thackeray studied law and Dickens became a reporter, a job which took him frequently to the law courts in London.

By far the happiest times of Thackeray's life were the many holidays he spent at Fareham with his great-grandmother, Anne Beecher. At first these holidays were spent at her rented house in High Street, though she would later move to a cottage on the corner of West Street and Portland Street. This building was demolished in the 1930s to make way for the former bus station.

Thackeray's writings, prolific from the mid-1830s, included articles in the leading magazines of the day, pamphlets, essays and short stories. His satiric genius was already well-developed in the collection known as *The Book of Snobs*. Novels in serial form followed, of which *Vanity Fair*, his undoubted masterpiece, appeared in instalments in 1847/8 and was an immediate success. Even today the satirical, sometimes cruel, humour, adulterous relationships and family rivalries amaze and delight readers. In *Vanity Fair*, Thackeray even manages to look back on

William Makepeace Thackeray – a sketch by Daniel Maclise.

his late father's career; the character of Jos Sedley, the rather stupid brother of Becky Sharpe's friend, Amelia, is employed by the East India Company as a Collector for Boggley Wallah.

Thackeray's marriage was not a happy one. His wife, Isabella, who became mentally ill after the birth of their third child, was confined in various institutions, possibly suffering a severe form of post-natal depression, a condition not recognised in the pre-Freudian era.

Shortly before his early death in 1863, Thackeray was editor of the prestigious *Cornhill Magazine*, in which he typically wrote comic pieces and short stories incognito. He predeceased Dickens by just seven years. His view of Fareham, which stayed with him throughout his life, was as a kind of haven of peace and small-town simplicity. This is expressed in the essay 'A Peal of Bells', which describes the house in High Street. He delighted in its sloping roof, its narrow porch, its flower garden leading to the road and its long back garden leading down to the River Wallington.

Best of all, surely, is Thackeray's recollection of Fareham as:

> ... a dear little old Hampshire town inhabited by the wives, widows and daughters of navy captains, admirals and lieutenants.

It is perhaps not a description we would recognise today!

William of Wykeham (1324–1404)

The Bishop best known for his motto 'Manners Maketh Man' came from a humble family in Wickham, Hampshire. His father, John Long, was variously described as a man of free condition, or as a serf, probably a labourer, working for the lord of the local manor. Although William was recognised from an early age as a clever child, the family's very limited means precluded them from giving him an education. He seems to have caught the eye of two members of the Hampshire gentry, Sir Ralph Sutton, Constable of Winchester Castle, and Sir John Saires, Lord of the Manor of Wickham. Sutton, possibly the young William's first employer, also helped to train him. By his early twenties, he is described as a chaplain, meaning an unbeneficed clerk.

William of Wykeham's knowledge of building and surveying won him the post of Chief Keeper and Surveyor of the castles at Windsor, Leeds (in Kent), Dover and Hadleigh, as well as the responsibility for new building works at Queenborough on the Isle of Sheppey. This particular appointment is regarded as a model for his later office as Clerk of the King's Works. By this period of his life, William had acquired a depth of knowledge and discernment regarding the quality of architecture and artefacts that would be important in his later life, when he became a founder, patron and benefactor of the arts and education.

From 1361 onwards, William's career became increasingly political. Appointed Edward III's Royal Secretary, he was involved in high-level negotiations with, and on behalf of, the king. His modern equivalent might be a spin-doctor or influential press secretary with the king's ear. All monarchical business was done through him. The French chronicler Froissart neatly summed up William's hold over the king and his ministers: 'Everything was done by him and without him nothing was done.'

It is clear that William of Wykeham was no divinely inspired priest or ancient theologian. He was primarily a clever and ambitious man who used his many skills to work in his favour with the great and the powerful. Edward III made him Bishop of Winchester, his enthronement taking place on 9 July 1368 when he was 44. A year later he was Chancellor of England. Unlike another bishop, Thomas à Becket, also a political figure, William of Wykeham weathered many storms during a long life. At one time, he was charged with treason but clearly had the true politician's ability to talk himself out of trouble.

The last 20 years of William's life were, perhaps, the most glorious in achievement. His prime enthusiasm being for education, he instigated the construction of New College, Oxford. Work began in March 1380 and was finally completed on 14 April 1386, when the first scholars were admitted. Work on Winchester College, also founded by William, began in March 1387, its first scholars being enrolled in 1395. The high standard of construction in these two colleges evidences the fact that the now elderly bishop was a man both wealthy and with an aesthetic appreciation of fine architecture.

William of Wykeham lived and worked through the reigns of Edward III, Richard II and Henry IV. One of the principal patrons of the arts during his long life, he has been called 'the father of the public school system'. This lowly Wickham boy knew instinctively the benefits of education as a means of advancement. William died at South Waltham, Hampshire, on 27 September 1404 in his eightieth year. His magnificent tomb, in the chantry of Winchester Cathedral, bears tribute to his importance to society in medieval England.

The Fontley forge and mill, where Cort carried out his experiments.

The Weathervane Ship stands outside Woolworth's, as summer shoppers come and go among the items of street furniture designed by blacksmith Charles Normandale for the Henry Cort exhibition, pictured here in June 2005.

Bibliography

Alexander, Eric (2000) *West Street Trail*, Wroughtware Publications
Aylott, Robert (1981) *Fareham: Two Views*, Front Page Books Ltd
Brown, Ron (1983) *The Fareham Of Yesteryear*, Milestone Publications
Burgess, Anthony (1972) *Shakespeare*, Penguin
Burton L. and Musselwhite B. (1991) *An Illustrated History Of Fareham*, Ensign Publications
Clark, Alan (ed.) (1974) *A Good Innings: The Private Papers of Viscount Lee Of Fareham*, John Murray
Cox, Trevor, *The History Of Locks Heath*
Emery, John (1985) *Fareham In Old Picture Postcards*, European Library
The Fareham Society (1995) *Fareham Town Walks*, The Fareham Society
Hughes, Michael (1976) *The Small Towns Of Hampshire*, Hampshire CC
Jacobs, Arthur (1984) *Arthur Sullivan*, Oxford University Press
James, Alice (1989) *Fareham Between The Wars*, Paul Cave Publications
James, Alice (1991) *Our Beloved Fareham*, Paul Cave Publications
James, Alice (1996) *The Archive Photo Series: Fareham*, Chalford
James, Alice (1998) *Around Fareham: The Second Selection*, Tempus
Jones, Peter (1981) *Eighteen Churches In The Alverstoke Deanery*, Calenor Ltd
Le Faye, D. *Jane Austen's Letters*, Oxford University Press, 1998.
Light, F.W. (1995) *A Short History Of Warsash*, Warsash Nautical Bookshop
Lloyd, David (1974) *The Buildings Of Portsmouth And Its Environs*, Portsmouth CC
Low, Malcolm (2003) *The Red Lion Hotel, Fareham: A History*, Malcolm Low
Miller, Patrick (1981) *Provincial – The Gosport And Fareham Story*, Transport Publishing Co.
Mitchell V. and Smith K. (1989) *Fareham To Salisbury Via Eastleigh*, Middleton Press
Montgomery, Alan (1987), *Tom, Tom, The Farmer's Son*, Alan Montgomery
Moore, Pamela (1984) *Industrial Heritage Of Hampshire and The Isle Of Wight*, Phillimore
Moore, Pamela (1990) *Bygone Fareham*, Phillimore
Morris, Christopher (1984) *Rural Rides By William Cobbett: Selections From The Writings*, Webb & Bower
Palmer, Oonagh (1998) *Around Fareham 1898–1998*, Sutton Publishing Ltd
Price, D. et al. (1998) *A Century Of Music – The History Of The Fareham Philharmonic Society*, Fareham Philharmonic Society
Privett, George (1949) *The Story Of Fareham*, Warren & Son
Read, D.H.M. (1908) *Highways And Byways In Hampshire*, MacMillan
Robertson, B.J. (1989) *Around Portsmouth Harbour*, Apex
Rowse, A.L. (1965) *Shakespeare's Southampton*, MacMillan
Stephenson, Michael (2004) *Fareham Revisited* and *Fareham Revisited Again*, Michael Stephenson
Titchfield History Society (1987) *Titchfield – A History*, Titchfield History Society
Titchfield History Society (1989) *Titchfield – A Place In History*, Titchfield History Society

The following papers are to be found in the Hampshire Record Office:
The History And Development Of Knowle Hospital, 1852–1992, by Peter Tunks
History of Knowle Hospital, 1852–1884, by R. Barsell
Admission Books And Registers Of The Hampshire Lunatic Asylum, 1832–1870
The Knowle Hospital Experience: Written and Researched by C. Attard, D. Brown, R. Chatterton, P. Conway, D. Short, D. Steele and C. White

Other Works Consulted:
Fareham Borough Council Official Guide Books
Fareham Local History Group, 1960–2005
Fareham Past And Present, the magazines of the Westbury Manor Museum Document Collection
Hampshire Magazine, 1960–2005
Kelly's Directories 1899, 1937, 1959, 1975
Pigott's Directory for Fareham, 1792 and 1798
Post Office Directory for Hants, Wilts and Dorset 1875
Southampton Evening Echo
The News, Portsmouth

Subscribers

E.J. and R.F. Abbatt, Titchfield, Hampshire
M.E. Abraham, Fareham, Hampshire
Ernest W. Adams, Locksheath, Hampshire
Ann and Fred, Fareham
Glenda and Nigel Ashdown-Watts, Fareham, Hampshire
Pam and Bill Bailey, Alexander Grove, Fareham
Mrs Pamela Bailey
Mr Bob Bailey
Mrs Eileen Bailey (née Scrase)
Janet M. Bainbridge, Fareham, Hampshire
Kevin M. Bainbridge, Fareham, Hampshire
Christine Carole Barnes
Brenda A. Barrett, Orchard Lea, Fareham
Mr Roger Barrett, Fareham, Hampshire
Kenneth J.E. Bates, Gosport, Hampshire
John H. Best, Portsmouth, Hampshire
Laurence W. Bishop, Fareham, Hampshire
Paul and Jacqueline Blaker, Fareham
Kay Boyes
The Boyle Family, Fareham
Mr Andrew Brookes
Pamela J. Brown (née Ledbury), Fareham, Hampshire
Mr and Mrs M.F. Bryant
David and Brenda Bullimore, Fareham, Hampshire
Chris Bushell, Fareham, Hampshire
Andrew M. Buxcey, Portchester, Hampshire
David A. Buxcey, Fareham, Hampshire
Mr James A. Carpenter, Fareham, Hampshire
Mr Brian R. Carter, Fareham, Hampshire
Godfrey A. Cave, Fareham, Hampshire
George J. Channon, Fareham, Hampshire
Ron, Nicolette and Chloe Chivers
Carol and Eric Clarke, Fareham
Linda S. Coles, Fareham, Hampshire
Angela Joan Collings (née Hare), Fareham
Sidney Albert and Raymond Albert Collins, Fareham, Hampshire
Mr William Cooper, Fareham, Hampshire
Florence D. Corbishley, Fareham, Hampshire
Derek and Marian Corke, Fareham, Hampshire
Frank and Ada Cottle, Fareham, Hampshire
Peter Charles Crofts, Portchester, Fareham
Mr N. Curtis, Fareham, Hampshire
Myrtle and Alan Dade, Fareham
Josephine May Dale, Fareham, Hampshire
Gilbert Dash, Fareham
A.G.R. and P. Dawkins
Richard Henry Deacon
Brian J. Dodge, Fareham Woodcarvers

✤ SUBSCRIBERS ✤

Lee J. Downer, Fareham, Hampshire
Robert and Geraldine Durrant, Valle-Mar, Hunters Lodge, Catisfield, Fareham
Charles W. Ellis, Fareham, Hampshire
Mrs Rosemary E. Evill (née Allen), Fareham, Hampshire
Michael George Fay
Mr Derek J. Forder, Fareham, Hampshire
Bertram W. Francis, Fareham, Hampshire
Jim Fraser, Hornet Sailing Club
Mr John Garrett M.Inst.L.M. and Mrs Evelene E.G. Garrett, Fareham
Robert K. Gasser, Gosport, Hampshire
Rita Gedge (née Strugnell), Fareham, Hampshire
William T.J. George, Fareham, Hampshire
Phyllis M. Gilbert
Robert Henry Goodman
Margaret and Graham E. Goss
Joan and Cliff Greatrex, Gosport
Alan Green, Swanmore, Hampshire
Mr Dave and Mrs Kim Hancock, Stubbington, Fareham
Linda M. Handover, Fareham, Hampshire
Mr John W. Hardman, Fareham, Hampshire
Ken Harrison
Wilfred Harvey-White, Titchfield
Mr F.T. Haughey, Fareham, Hampshire
Lynne Hitchins, Fareham, Hampshire
Daphne Hobbs, Fareham, Hampshire
John Hobbs, Poole, Dorset
Lorraine D. Hoile (née Dean), Fareham, Hampshire
Jean M. Hopkins, Fareham, Hampshire
David G. Horscroft
Pamela K. Hunt, Titchfield, Fareham, Hampshire
Mr and Mrs T. Johns, Southwick, Hampshire
Allan H. Jones, Fareham, Hampshire
Janice Judd, Fareham, Hampshire
Michael Keith-Smith FRICS
Eric W. King-Turner, Titchfield, Hampshire
Roy Kingswell, Fontley
Barry and Judy Lang, Fareham, Hampshire
Arthur L. Leach, Titchfield, Hampshire
Pat Lee (née Nicholson), Gosport, Hampshire
Veronica E. Lee, Fareham, Hampshire
Steve Leisching, formerly Fareham/now Sussex
Mrs Margaret Lugg, Chairman of Fareham West T.G.
F.J. Matthews, Fareham, Hampshire
R.S. Matthews
Sylvia and John McDermid
Stephen McGrath, Putney, London
Raymond and Frances Mills, Fareham, Hampshire
Joan and Bill Mitchell, Fareham
Robert I. Montague, Fareham, Hampshire
Gemma Kate Moss, Fareham, Hampshire
Hannah Jane Moss, Fareham, Hampshire
Charles, Claire and William Musselwhite, Swanage, Dorset
Johanna Noonan (née McGrath), Gosport, Hampshire
Mr and Mrs P. and S. O'Sullivan, Fareham, Hampshire

Stephen G. Osborne, Fareham
Julie Palmer (née Spanner), Fareham, Hampshire
Mrs Peggy Pannell
Derek E. Pattle, Fareham, Hampshire
Mr Michael J. Pellatt, Stubbington, Hampshire
Kathleen M. Pottinger, Fareham, Hampshire
John and Pam Press, Fareham, Hampshire
John C. Prout
Shirley and Mike Rees, Fareham, Hampshire
Phyllis E. Riches
Sally P. Riordan, Queensland, Australia
Audrey Rogers
Angela Rowsell, Fareham, Hampshire
Charles T. Roy, West End, Hampshire
David Rymill, Winchester, Hampshire
Mr and Mrs R.W. Sanderson
Pauline Saxey (née Moody), Titchfield Common, Fareham
Jean Shannon, Fareham, Hampshire
Reginald E. Sharp, Fareham, Hampshire
Mrs Julia P. Simkin, Fareham, Hampshire
Kathleen J. Simmonds, Fareham, Hampshire
Martin and Sandra Smallwood, Fareham, Hampshire
John, Judith, Sean and Darren Snelgar, Fareham, Hampshire
Mr and Mrs W. Stacey
Brian and Diane Stevens, Fareham, Hampshire
Mrs Cecilia Stickland, Fareham, Hampshire
J. Strugnell, Wallington, Fareham, Hampshire
Roy B. Talbot, Fareham, Hampshire
Mr Paul B. Taylor, Fareham, Hampshire
David Turner and Marie-Eve Noel, Fareham
Patricia E. Walker, Fareham, Hampshire
Mrs Rona Walker (née Coombes), Fareham
Valerie Walker, Fareham, Hampshire
John F.W. Walling, Newton Abbot, Devon
June S. Ward, Fareham, Hampshire
Michael J. Warren, Fareham, Hampshire
Kathleen Joyce West
Eddie John Whicker and Katharine Hole
Mrs Anne M. White (née Simpson), Portchester
Judith Anne Whitear, Fareham, Hampshire
J. Wilde, Fareham
David A. Wilkinson, Fareham, Hampshire
Mrs Jean Wilson (née Cook), Fareham
Jeane Withers, Fareham, Hampshire
David V.J. Wright, Fareham, Hampshire
Mrs Rosina M. Wright, Fareham, Hampshire
Mr Chris Wyatt, Titchfield, Fareham
Lynda Young, Fareham, Hampshire

There are now over 160 titles in the Community History Series. For a full listing of these and other Halsgrove publications, please visit www.halsgrove.com or telephone 01884 243 242